WHY PICK ON ME?
School exclusion and Black youth

WHY PICK ON ME?
School exclusion and Black youth
Maud Blair

Trentham Books

Stoke on Trent, UK and Sterling, USA

Trentham Books Limited

Westview House	22883 Quicksilver Drive
734 London Road	Sterling
Oakhill	VA 20166-2012
Stoke on Trent	USA
Staffordshire	
England ST4 5NP	

First published 2001

British Library Cataloguing-in-Publication Data
A catalogue record for this book is available from the British Library

ISBN 1 85856 231 7

Designed and typeset by Trentham Print Design Ltd., Chester and printed in Great Britain by Cromwell Press Ltd., Wiltshire.

Contents

Dedication

For my children, Michael, Marti and Joanna

It's like it ain't so much what a fellow does, but it's the way the
majority of folks is looking at him when he does it.
(William Faulkner – *As I Lay Dying*)

Acknowledgements

This book would not have been possible without the help and co-operation of head-teachers, teachers, school governors and other staff, students and their parents. To all those who allowed me into their schools, their homes and their hearts, I am very grateful.

I was sustained throughout this project and during the research and writing of my thesis on which this book is largely based by a number of people. Peter Woods, Kathy Stredder, Audrey Osler, David Gillborn, Chris Searle, Steven Small, Julia Sudbury and the Women's Leadership Institute, Mills College, California, were vital lifelines during the work on my thesis.

For the book itself, I received unstinting support and encouragement from my children, Michael, Marti and Joanna, my sister Margaret Crofts, friends Robin Richardson and Rodney and Caroline Blair.

Paul Boyd, Kamari Clarke and Julia Sudbury gave me valuable feedback. Thank you.

A special mention has to be made of my friend Basil Williams who made it possible for me to stay with his mother, and 'of course', 'Ma' Elizabeth Williams who opened her home to me and gave me months of peace and quiet in St Vincent and the Grenadines.

June Evison at the Open University has been a rock throughout, no matter where in the world I have been. My colleagues at the Centre for Sociology and Social Research at the OU, and in particular Liz Dawtrey, Merril Hammer, Patricia Murphy and Kathy Stredder without whose support and co-operation I could not have gone away for so long.

Importantly, I want to thank Gillian Klein, John Stipling and the staff at Trentham Books for their patience and efficiency, Gillian's meticulous editing is second to none. To everyone of you, my sincere thanks.

1

Introduction

During a visit to St Vincent and the Grenadines, a friend and I were discussing whether boys really do underachieve in schools in the Caribbean and elsewhere, or whether this was in fact a myth. The discussion inevitably went to the underachievement of black[1] students in British schools and the contributory factor of racism. My friend told me that he was so glad that he had chosen to raise his daughter in the Caribbean because, as he said, 'She will never know what it is to have such an experience in school. As far as she is concerned, the world is her oyster. She doesn't have any of that stuff to contend with'.

I listened to my friend with some envy. Racism had never not been part of my or my children's experience. Growing up in segregated Rhodesia, my life and that of my family had always been circumscribed by race[2]. I went to England to escape the more virulent forms of racial differentiation, or so I thought, only to encounter racism like an itch which would not go away. Sometimes the 'spot' was obvious and you could scratch at it directly. But other times, for example in employment, you felt the itch but when you tried to scratch, it seemed to move and you could not pin it down. You simply lived with its constant irritation. As a young mother and a new immigrant I remember the helplessness I felt in the face of my son's experience of racial harassment. I felt as if I had violated some British standard of decency by displaying the chip which I was told I carried on my shoulder every time I tried to discuss his unhappiness.

To return to the discussion I was having with my friend, I tried to imagine what the experience of school for black children in Britain might be like if only they could be allowed to learn in the kind of environment he described. This is not to claim that the history of St Vincent and the Grenadines (SVG) and other parts of the Caribbean is not a history of racism, or that racism is not manifest in subtle forms or in absences, for example of African history in the curriculum. Neither does it mean that students at SVG schools escape other forms of social exclusion based on, for example, social class or gender. But the mention of racism to students in SVG produced blank stares – they did not identify its different forms as factors in their own country which affected their ability to learn, to achieve or as an obstacle to their life's ambitions.

Yet my own and others' discussions with black students in schools in Britain indicate that racism – especially if it comes from teachers – produces in them the strongest feelings of helplessness. Not that they cannot retaliate or in turn create problems for the perpetrator, but helpless in the way that it cuts deeply into their sense of who they are, their place in and value to society. But what kind of change would British society have to go through before black and other minority students could feel as their white counterparts do that racism was one less obstacle to contend with? My studies of school suspensions and expulsions (exclusion[3]) left me feeling less than optimistic. But there was room for optimism when I considered some of the emancipatory changes that have taken place in some schools, albeit few. I also thought that in all the years I have worked in schools in Britain, and in all my interviews and talks with white teachers, I have come across very few who did not seem to have a genuine concern and caring for all their students of whatever background.

After three, four and in some cases more, generations of black children going through the British education system, however, so little seems to have changed. On the question of exclusion from the education system alone, Bernard Coard (1971) had documented the horrendous practice in the 1960s and 1970s of confining disproportionate numbers of black children into disciplinary units or 'sin-

2

bins'. The over-representation of black students in exclusion from school today is clearly not an effect of the 1988 Education Reform Act but goes deep into the history of education in Britain (Blair and Cole, 2000). This is an important point because if we assume that the problem of exclusion faced by black students is the direct effect of market principles, then it could also be assumed that the removal of such principles and practices would end these problems. What would in fact happen is that the problem of exclusion might reduce for white students to pre-1988 figures, but would simply render invisible once again the unacceptable levels of exclusion from school for black students. What the 'market' has done is to exacerbate the problem of exclusion of black students. At the time of writing this book, black students in certain local education authorities were *nineteen* times more likely to be excluded than their white counterparts (CRE, 2000).

Why should students be excluded at all at the present rates, and why should black students experience such disproportionate levels of exclusion? This is what I wish to explore in this book. In doing so, I draw on my experience as a former Advisory Teacher for Multicultural Education, and on a number of research projects carried out over the years, four studies in particular. One, which was commissioned by Barnardos and the Family Service Units, was on the effects on working class families of expelling children from school. The second was a study of effective multi-ethnic schools commissioned by the Department for Education and Employment (DfEE), the third was on the over-representation of black students in school exclusions which I carried out for my doctoral thesis (PhD) and the fourth a study of exclusions in two schools commissioned by the Education Mediation Service of a London Borough (LEA). The studies will be referred to throughout the book by these acronyms. All were qualitative, employing mainly interviews as the research tool. Through these experiences of research and teaching, I want to explore a number of questions which, while they may have no easy answers, might help to illuminate some of the issues in our schools and, at the very least, stimulate discussion and critical reflection among teachers.

What is Exclusion?

We need to clarify the meaning of the term exclusion. Officially it is used by the DfEE to mean suspension and expulsion from school. However, exclusion from the educational process and from constructive schooling has gone on and continues in many different forms in schools. Children from all kinds of backgrounds and experiences are routinely excluded. As Booth *et al* (1997:338) declare,

> All schools respond to the diversity of their students with a mixture of including and excluding measures, in terms of who they admit to the school, how students are categorised, grouped and disciplined, how teaching and learning is organised, how resources are used, how students who experience difficulties are supported, and how curricula and teaching is developed so that such difficulties are reduced.

Fine (1991: 26), referring to the American context, contends that exclusion

> so thoroughly saturates public schooling, at least in low income urban areas, that it requires no malevolence, no 'bad guys', no conspiracy.

Several writers in Britain have discussed the different ways in which ethnicity and race function to exclude minority ethnic groups from constructive participation in the education system and from society generally. Wright (1987) for example, wrote about the exclusion of black students from those bands, sets and streams which allow students to meet their educational potential. Black students were, instead, confined to the areas of the curriculum which destroyed motivation and guaranteed lower qualifications or failure (see also Oakes, 1985; Goodlad, 1984). Mac an Ghaill (1988), Gillborn (1990), Mirza (1992), Connolly (1995), amongst others, have written about the assumptions and practices of teachers which exclude students on the basis of their class, gender, sexuality and ethnicity. Many others have described the exclusion of students on the basis of their disability, learning needs, language and religion.

It is important not to confine the term exclusion to disciplinary measures alone, but that we understand this broader meaning. There are three reasons. First, such an understanding helps us recognise that many children from different groups are vulnerable, and forces us to place the exclusion of black students in the context of wider experiences of social injustice and inequality. It is now well documented that the overwhelming majority of students who are suspended or expelled are from working class or poor homes, are in 'looked after' situations, or involved with the social services in some way (SEU, 1998; Hayden, 1997; OFSTED, 1996; Cohen *et al.* 1994; Bourne *et al.* 1994; DFE, 1993). It is clear that whatever has led to this situation affects the most vulnerable children in our schools. It can be argued, however, that black students *generally* but not *necessarily* fit these different categories and this seems to indicate that racism also has its own powerful dynamic which leads to such different outcomes for students, even when controlling for gender and class (Gillborn, 1995b; OFSTED, 1996). It is difficult otherwise to explain why black working class boys/girls should receive more criticism and punishment than white working class boys and girls who commit the same 'offences' (cf Gillborn 1990).

But by placing the problems faced by black students in a broader social as well as historical perspective, we can avoid the reductionism that can result from a focus on racism alone in the experience of black students. This understanding might also help us to avoid attempted solutions of the kind so roundly condemned by the Macdonald Report (1989) on the murder of Ahmed Iqbal Ullah at Burnage High School in Manchester. Although Burnage High School was largely vilified for its focus on antiracism to the exclusion of the other social and political factors which impact on the lives of all – and not only black – students, their policies were nevertheless a recognition of the detrimental effects of racism. But such dubious solutions arise when we operate from the premise that there is only one problem to be tackled and that that problem affects only one category of students. By addressing more broadly the systems of exclusion within education generally and the way that schools as institutions conduct their business, we are more likely to see that the problems which confront black students are rooted in an interplay of social factors of which racism is only one, albeit the one which arouses the most emotion in black students and their families and communities and is probably also the most dangerous.

The second reason for looking more broadly at the systems of exclusion operating in schools has to do with teachers. Education and
the processes of schooling weigh upon the identities of not only
students but also of teachers. Teachers cannot correct the de-
ficiencies of the system – to the extent that it is within their power
to do so, and I believe this power to be greater than we generally
accept – if they are constantly taking a defensive position in relation
to their personal and professional identities. The notion that the
problems that beset black students are entirely caused by racism
presents white teachers as uniformly or generally racist and this is
taken to imply that they are somehow deficient as human beings and
unprofessional as teachers. This interpretation is based of course on
a poor understanding of how racism operates. More disturbing, it
can prevent or block a proper understanding in *teachers themselves*
of their function within a school system which categorises and
separates students in various ways. It can prevent teachers from seeing how they contribute to this process when they conduct 'business
as usual' and fail to adopt a critical and reflective approach which
would enable them to empathise with their students and be more
consciously compassionate in their dealings with them. Instead of
allowing space for teachers to examine their identities as *white*[4]
people and what that means in terms of their world views and perspectives, it pushes them into a defensive position which stymies
such personal reflection.

A third effect of focusing exclusively on racism as the cause of exclusion of black students is that it encourages the divisiveness
created by 'ethnic absolutism', a term used by Gilroy (1992) to describe a particular mode of identity politics used by black people to
justify separate ethnic enclaves. I fear that ethnic absolution can also
be used as a way of 'othering' black people. This happens when
black people or students are seen as so distinctive that what becomes
most obvious about them are the differences of that group from
others. The commonalities that exist in humankind are obscured.
This creates a mental blockage about 'them' whereby 'they' become
a mystery to 'us' and 'we' then lose all sense of this group of
students as children, boys, girls, adolescents, and so on and their

ethnicity remains the main or even sole definer of their identities. 'We' then find 'ourselves' unable to address 'their' needs and concerns. Wright *et.al* (2000), for example, report how one teacher felt that black children were so different that she did not know how to deal with them. There is something intellectually and spiritually barren about anyone, let alone a teacher, who, in the twenty-first century, can only see skin colour and cannot see the human being behind the skin – and a child at that.

Such antiquated views are probably not unusual. They are part of a cultural and historical legacy which continues not only because many of the teachers in our schools have had very little contact with 'ethnic difference' in both their upbringing and training but also because they continue to have little if any knowledge of their students' lives outside of school. Government policies and teacher education institutions do little to change the normative world views, which appear to have undergone little evolutionary change since Victorian times. But there is more to this perspective than simply not having personal knowledge of students. When black children are in fact British and have therefore absorbed many of the cultural and customary habits of the British, when they speak English, the country's language of cultural understanding and communication, and when so many today have one white parent, why should the melanin content of their skins be the basis on which they are judged and the sole means by which they are understood and their needs assessed? This perception that black children are somehow mysterious, unknowable, brings to mind Ralph Ellison (1965) when he said

> When they approach me they see only my surroundings, themselves, or figments of their imagination – indeed everything and anything except me...That invisibility to which I refer occurs because of a peculiar disposition of the eyes of those with whom I come in contact. A matter of the construction of their *inner* eyes, those eyes with which they look through their physical eyes upon reality. (p.5)

The problem is a problem of the inner eye. It is a vision of a reality which draws on history, on culture, on knowledge passed down from one generation to another, carried through the main arteries of a nation's information systems, and whose central features enter the psyche of whole groups or nations with but minor alteration. Without deep personal reflection on how we have come by our particular worldviews and how these affect our interactions with the world, there is little room for change at either an individual or group level. The racial legacy of Europe generally and of Britain's specific historical relations with many parts of the world can still be found in our schools today. But this is only one part of the story. Alongside it runs the feeling – and I can put it no stronger than that – that 'their' ways are not 'our' ways and 'they' need to be made to conform to 'our' way of doing things. Given the diversity of backgrounds of black children and the number of years black children have attended British schools, this is a total myth, a construction which perpetuates the notion that black students need greater surveillance and control than white students. There is thus very little change in the basic narrative of Britain's racialised history. It has simply shifted at different points and in particular situations. While there may be more awareness of racism, there is still little analytical understanding of how racism operates in different ways and in different contexts.

It could be argued that racialised views and attitudes are not 'racist' in the *malicious* sense but that their effects are what matter. I argue in the next section, for example, that 'intention' is not the sole definer of racism. These views and attitudes are the result of seeing the world through an unexamined inner eye, a conventional wisdom which is indicative not necessarily of the individual's motives but of her or his life experience. Studies of race and education have indicated that much of the racism operating in schools is not deliberate or overt, but takes place at an unconscious level (Gillborn, 1995a; Mac an Ghaill,1988; King, 1998) or is part of the taken-for-granted, 'common sense', everyday ways in which (white) teachers make sense of the world (Sleeter, 1996; Essed, 1990). It is important therefore that we find ways of dealing with unintentional forms of racism and recognising their damaging effects whilst also differentiating them from blatant or malicious acts.

Racism, Motive and Identity

The issue of motive is often a sticking point when it comes to discussions of racism in schools. Because a teacher's intentions are not malicious, it is often assumed that the fault lies with the 'chip on the shoulder' of the person who experiences a particular interaction as racist. One could find many examples of this in schools. I will provide one which for me illustrates the complex relationship between the inner eye, motive and identity.

A fourteen year old black girl was particularly restless in class one day. She walked about to the waste basket, to borrow things from others, to look out the window, and finally – for reasons not explained to me – she stood on her chair. The teacher, exasperated, said, 'Would you sit down and stop climbing on the furniture. It makes you look like a monkey'. The girl, shocked, kicked her chair over and walked out of the classroom. She was of course suspended.

It is easy enough to empathise with the teacher who was trying to do his job of educating his students and having to deal with the disruptive influences of a restless student. I won't question here whether his lesson was sufficiently interesting to keep his students engaged. The point is that both drew on their long historical memories, one for the analogy, and the other for the reaction to the analogy. The teacher had no intention, as he strongly protested, of being racist to the student. He would, as he said, have used the example of the monkey regardless of the race of the student. This may of course be true, but one cannot dismiss the possibility that his memory, both ancient and lived, in other words his inner eye was more likely to convey messages of a monkey to his visual eye *because* the student was black. His intention, as he said, had little to do with it. It had a great deal to do with his identity and history as a white person. The student, on the other hand, was drawing on her long ancestral, as well as lived, memory of racial categorisation and insult, in particular the association of black people with monkeys, and justifiably felt racially abused by the teacher's remark. The student's sense of justice was that she was doubly punished while the teacher was let off without having to apologise, all because he had not *intended* to abuse her.

Should the teacher have been reprimanded for his part in what happened? Perhaps, but the focus should be more on education and less on punishment. But neither should the student have been suspended. The teacher needed to be reminded of the significance of particular images in the racialistion of society – and was already aware of the significance of the monkey in racist discourses – and to acknowledge and apologise for his mistake, his intentions notwithstanding. Indeed an ability to accept responsibility for his part in the problem should have formed part of his initial teacher education and of in-service training in the school. The student, on the other hand, needed to be *reminded* about how to respond to such insults – reminded because such information should already have been laid down in the school's Code of Practice for students *and* teachers. The incident would probably not have escalated had such a Code of Practice existed, detailing how students and teachers should react to problems in the classroom.

When the personal is professional

All human beings want to safeguard their personal identities. This is as true of teachers as it is of the students they teach. Teachers are also concerned to preserve their professional identities. Accusations of racism, implying an intention to hurt in some way, violate teachers' sense of themselves as people and as professionals. Yet there seems to be little understanding of how this can be taken into account in dealing with problems in schools, without at the same time underplaying the seriousness of racism. Those who are likely to suffer as a result are the students, because the same practices are repeated, either because teachers feel affronted by such accusations and so pay no attention to what they really mean or why they have been made, or because they simply do not understand the basis of the accusation and are too scared to ask in case this merely confirms to everyone that they are racist. Those of us who have tried to raise equality issues on committees will be familiar with the exasperated lifting of eyebrows from some members who think that we are raising these issues not because they matter and we would like them taken seriously but because we are merely on an egotistical 'political correctness' trip. We also know how paralysing such dismissals can be. Similarly, some teachers feel unable to move forward in their understanding of the discursive practices of race because the silent responses or looks of exasperation they receive when they raise a question seem to be asking, 'what planet are you from?' or saying, 'no wonder black children have a problem'.

After such a long history of migration to Britain from the former colonies, there should be no excuse for teachers not knowing or understanding about race and racism. But after nine years of teaching a unit on race mainly to teachers, and four years in a leading teacher training college in Britain, I am convinced that when it comes to understanding about race, and about how racisms operate, many of the teachers who go into schools year in year out are out of touch with the realities of the students they will teach and can indeed be the source of many of the problems faced by black students. Imagine the problems that can be created by essentialising statements such as, 'Our black boys are so well co-ordinated that it is better to focus on their gift for sport than try to force them to do subjects which they find so boring and difficult' – a statement which a teacher told me had been made by a Section 11[5] teacher. This is not far from saying that black students are so different that white teachers would not know how to cater for them.

The question is, however, how to move teachers from this position. How do we create a better understanding of diversity, of difference, and of the corrosive effects of racism? We certainly cannot expect teachers to listen with open minds unless we approach the topic in a manner which leaves their sense of integrity intact. On the other hand, statements from students, especially secondary school students, indicate that many teachers equally do not consider the personal identities of students in their dealings with them. Something is wrong with a teacher education service which leaves teachers so woefully ill-prepared for a career in a context which has clearly changed from largely mono-ethnic to multi-ethnic, multi-faith and multilingual. Chapter 5 describes how black students felt demeaned as human beings in their individual dealings with teachers.

We seldom hear of the effects of social class on the routine activities of school. Yet this too needs to be understood and to form part of the professional education that teachers receive. Teachers need to understand the extent to which the 'inner eye' on issues of race is linked to the social class culture and history of Britain. The inner eye provides not only a racialised vision of the world, it also creates a particular orientation in the teacher in social class terms. This has its roots in the class divisions of the society and also in the specific history of education in Britain. Although student teachers are generally familiarised with this history, seldom are they asked to reflect on their identities as (white) middle class professionals and ask themselves how this might affect their dealings with (black) working class students. One teacher told me that she did not take the 'multicultural option' at College because, as someone who had been born and raised in Africa, she had not thought she needed it. She had the grace to admit later that she probably needed that kind of education as much, if not more, than her colleagues.

Much more work has been done and continues to be done on gender, with studies reflecting on the gendered identities of both students and of teachers (Mirza, 1992; Walkerdine, 1989). Theorising white identity is a more recent phenomenon (Troyna, 1998; Delgado and Stephanic, 1997; Sleeter, 1996), as is an examination of the inter-actions of social class, gender and race on student experience (Wright *et.al* 2000).

In chapter 2, I examine the question of why, when teachers are in general caring and concerned people, they allow different kinds of social exclusion to occur in their schools. What are the processes which allow such inequalities to persist? I follow this in chapter 3 with a closer look at social constructions of children, and particularly black children, which help perpetuate such inequalities. I draw specifically on discourses of exclusion to illustrate some of the factors which lead to the exclusion of students and examine some of the human rights implications of removing young people from school.

This book is, however, largely about agency. It is about creating understanding, looking at possibilities and ways forward. By examining some of the attitudes and practices in our schools and suggesting alternative interpretations, I hope to create some understanding but also to show that those responsible for our children in schools can, both individually and collectively, produce significantly more positive results despite the obstacles and constraints. These issues are explored in chapter 4 through the role of the headteacher. As the only one who can exclude students from school, the headteacher holds a powerful position in relation to the future life chances of students. How deeply do headteachers think about this when they issue the papers removing a young person from the school? Do they consider what might happen to that person? Should they think about it? Do they in fact use permanent exclusion as a last resort, as the guidelines from the DfEE specify, or do they instead operate in response to the dictates of their staff? How much leadership do they show on this matter and what does leadership mean in this context? I explore the notion of 'orientation' to demonstrate the level of agency that headteachers have in deciding the route of a young person's life. Could a headteacher's orientation with regard to discipline, combined with the notion of the inner eye, highlight the disadvantaged position of black students in matters of discipline in schools?

Chapter 5 focuses on students. I discuss students' experience of school, their views on relationships with teachers and their perspectives on disciplinary processes. I compare and contrast these views with those of the teachers and explore the possibility that there might be a meeting point which allows teachers to exercise their authority without losing face, and allows students to feel respected, democratically involved and enabled to take responsibility for their own learning.

Chapter 6 examines what happens in relations between teachers and students and considers how much agency teachers have to prevent student exclusion. Can the poor interactions and bad relationships between teachers and black students detailed in so much of the literature be avoided? What are the factors that make for good relationships between teachers and students generally and between teachers and black students in particular? What questions ought teachers to ask and what changes might be needed in schools? To what extent does the 'inner eye' affect teachers' expectations of student behaviour and ability? I draw on the perspectives of teachers from several schools to explore the role of the peer group in influencing student behaviour. The concept of orientation will also be used to understand teacher perspectives on discipline.

In chapter 7 I introduce the perspectives of parents. Working class parents are often left in the margins of school life, on the assumption that they have little to contribute. The school is viewed, often by the parents themselves, as the domain of teachers. Social class, race and gender are a powerful combination in parents' experience of school. The experience of white parents of black children illustrates further the concept of the inner eye which, it is argued here, is not necessarily based on the skin colour nor the class position of the individual but rather on their association with black people. Theirs is a 'corrupted' whiteness which is both drawn from and reflected in their black children. Given that the parents are in fact the experts on their own children, I discuss possible ways in which they can become more involved in their children's schools. I argue, however, that the lack of involvement of parents should not of itself prevent caring and concern for even the most difficult of students.

Chapter 8 concludes by summarising the arguments presented in the book and indicating some ways forward. What might a more democratic school look like and how might it help create a better, more inclusive and less troubled ethos? I present some practical ideas for dealing with the issues raised in the book generally, concluding that as long as teachers believe in their students, they will have high expectations of them. And with high expectations come better relations and higher achievement. None of the suggestions are quick-fixes – but short-term sacrifices and efforts could reap some immediate and many long-term rewards.

Notes

1. I use the term 'black' to refer to peoples of African heritage, whether they are of African or Caribbean descent. I do not in this context use it to refer to students and teachers of South Asian descent, not because of the contested nature of this usage (see for example Modood, 1992), although I acknowledge this contestation, but because of the manner in which students (and teachers) have been ethnically categorized in the British school system. This categorisation is currently undergoing change. I mainly use the term exclusion but sometimes refer to suspension and expulsion for the sake of clarity in certain contexts.

2. Although often assumed to be natural and fixed, race is a contested category. For this reason, it often appears in text in inverted commas to signal its problematic nature. I have chosen to write it without the quotations marks as I believe that it is now widely understood to be a social construction.

3. The terms 'suspension' and 'expulsion' were replaced by the collective term exclusion by the Education Act (1986).

4. Approximately 98% of teachers in British schools are white. When I talk about teachers therefore, I mean white teachers, and will talk about 'black' teachers as and when the need arises.

5. Section 11 teachers were funded from a specific Home Office budget to help and support minority ethnic group children, especially those for whom English was an additional language. Section 11 funding has now been replaced by the Ethnic Minority Achievement Grant administered by the DfEE.

2

The education of teachers

Teacher education institutions generally ensure that their students are familiar with the history and development of education in Britain. Student teachers know that education was once seen as the monopoly of the elite social classes and that mass education was introduced in 1870. They will have been made familiar with the different theories of why mass education happened (though seldom about education in Britain's colonial empire). But history is often seen as a narrative of only the past. The continuities or the present consequences of past decisions are either not discussed or they are viewed from a scientific distance, as if they had nothing to do with real people. From my experience of teaching and from discussions with established, as well as newly qualified, teachers it seems to me that much of what student teachers learn is history so abstracted from what they will encounter in schools that they do not stop to consider just how much of the nineteenth century assumptions about the role of schools still underpin schooling today. Schools continue to function on the basis of nineteenth century assumptions about, for example, relationships between adults and children, and about the place of children, in a world where young people do not think or feel about the world or experience it as their nineteenth century counterparts did.

Students in schools, especially the older ones, no longer passively accept authority but function with an acute sense of their own rights, and will question or even challenge authority if they feel that those rights are at risk. We have with each generation failed to analyse the lives and expectations of students and devise constructive strategies for understanding and meeting their needs. Furthermore, students today will not simply accept their 'place' in society. In relation to the labour market, that place has shifted substantially from the coal mines or the docks or shipyards, and possibly even from the engineering and mechanical plants, to a world of unemployment and hopelessness. It is my view that disciplinary problems in schools are largely related to the inability of schools to connect with the changes that have taken place in the cultures of young people themselves and to understand their sense of rage and hopelessness, especially in poor urban areas. Students may be told that they come to school to gain qualifications in order to help them compete in the labour market, but they are only too aware that the labour market is gradually disappearing for people like themselves, who are in any case filtered out of the alleged economic benefits that education offers.

As for black students' relationship to the labour market in Britain, society may have allocated a temporary place for them in the backrooms and boiler rooms during the early part of the last century but, unlike the sons and daughters of miners, fishermen and secretaries, their parents had never accepted that they would be confined to one place (Bryan *et. al*, 1985). These early immigrants had dreams of the world as an oyster for their children. For most, these dreams have been shattered and what many of them have witnessed instead, are schools as hostile environments to both themselves and their children. For many young people, and for many young black people, school has no meaning. It is so divorced from their own lives, their hopes and aspirations, and their realistic assessment of their futures, that it means little more than a place of containment during their compulsory school years. A fifteen year old boy summed it up when he said to me, 'School is like doing time. I can't wait to get out of here'. School does not instil in them the notion of 'learning' as something desirable, enjoyable, rewarding, and for life. Black students in particular experience school as overly controlling, deaf to their needs, and diminishing of their sense of identity. Yet while black students feel increasingly marginalised because teachers work long hard hours to push what they see as 'profitable units' of students to achieve those A to C grades, many black parents continue to cling to the vague hope that however slight the benefits of schooling, their own children might be among the lucky ones to get a decent education and a decent job.

These are some of the important issues that are absent or barely touched upon in the preparation teachers receive for schooling now. Yet they do receive so much information that could help them understand better what the social aspects of their jobs as teachers entail. They are probably presented with the views of Marxists such as Bowles and Gintis (1976), who posit the class-based theory that schools are part of a wider political and economic plan to filter students for their role in the production of capital. They may be familiar with the view of neo-Marxists who support the idea that the economic systems of, for example, Britain and the USA are so organised that in order to generate high profit levels it is necessary for a certain amount of unemployment to be maintained in the society. Writers such as Apple (1990:36) say that this economic system 'is primarily concerned with the maximisation of the production of profit and only secondarily concerned with the distribution of resources and employment' (*op.cit.* p.43). The role of the school in such economies is to allocate people to the positions 'required' by the economic sector of society.

Student teachers will also probably have learnt that the hidden curriculum which is an effective means of filtering students through the schooling system can be found in the structures and practices of schools in capitalist economies of this type. Examples might be the middle class values that schools uphold and propound, the practices of setting and streaming children, the content of the school syllabus, and the system of examination. Giroux (1989:182) talks about how

> the hidden curriculum in school works in a subtly discriminatory way to discredit the dreams, experiences and knowledge associated with students from specific class, racial and gender groupings.

But are student teachers ever asked to examine what schools *should* be about and what their own beliefs and values are in relation to all this? Do they even make the connection between these various theories and the real live consequences for the students they are going to teach? Are they asked to consider who these class, racial and gender groupings might be in the real world? Are they asked to examine how this filtering process takes place and what their own roles in the process will be? Most importantly, do they examine why, if particular practices in schools lead to or create inequality, they take part in them? Do they make connections between schooling processes and their own identities as (white) middle class teachers? My discussions with teachers leave me convinced that teachers in training are not asked to make connections between these theories and real children in schools. Making connections between history, school processes and personal and professional identities is not encouraged and nor are they explicitly made. A newly qualified teacher in one primary school had this to say:

> When I started at this school I knew nothing about equal opportunities. Everything I know I learnt when I got here. On our course we had one lecture on race and although there was a multicultural option, I didn't do it because there were just so many things that seemed more urgent, like literacy and numeracy which had just been introduced into schools. I am lucky I came to this school which takes equal opportunities seriously because I know that a lot of my colleagues from college will go through their teaching career knowing very little about it.

The lack of preparedness of teachers is evident in teacher education institutions themselves, where black students report experiences of racism from tutors as well as fellow students (Siraj-Blatchford, 1991; Maylor, 1995). There is little, if any, discussion about how student teachers might themselves arrive at a better understanding of how racism confers privilege as well as disadvantage.

The important question still remains. Why do teachers, even after years of experience, fail to see the differentiating processes that take place in schools and to which they apparently contribute so willingly?

A number of writers have tried to find answers to this question. Whilst the Marxist view has been important in our understanding of why and how schools reproduce inequality, neo-Marxists argue that this view is not sufficient to explain why these inequalities should persist in the specific ways that they do (Giroux, 1989; Apple, 1988, 1990, 1996; Sharp and Green, 1984). It is an argument, they contend, which subsumes factors such as race and gender in class and which ignores the cultural dimension of social inequality. They see schools as instruments through which dominant groups maintain their control over less powerful groups, not because of a conspiracy among powerful people but through a system of *cultural hegemony*. By this they mean that the structures and curriculum of schools reflect and reproduce the cultural interests of dominant groups. The relationship, therefore, between the organisational structures of schools and the requirements of the economy is not a straight-forward one to one relationship. It is mediated by these cultural con-cerns which enter our taken-for-granted understandings of what schools have always been about and what they have traditionally done.

Schools are and have always been conservative places. But if the relationship between schools and the economic interests of dominant groups is not the result of a deliberate conspiracy on the part of those in power, how is it that caring, concerned human beings who have dedicated their lives to helping young people are taking part in excluding practices which can damage young people's lives? The argument is that dominant groups are able to maintain their power through *consensus* and schools function in a manner which reproduces inequality because of a consensus on what schools are about, what teachers should do, and what constitutes effectiveness. Hall (1984), drawing on the concept of hegemony as developed by Antonio Gramsci, states that the powerful are able to ensure that they continue to rule with the consent of the majority, if their own interests are closely allied to the interests of the majority.

The issue of exclusion generally and of disciplinary exclusions in particular, provides a graphic example of how consensus is built around the interests of dominant groups. This is discussed in the next chapter. It is important to state here that the cultural nature of the control exercised in schools means that schools become 'sites of struggle' (Hall, 1985) where the students do not passively accept what is dictated by the schools but struggle to keep their own cultural identities. Drawing on the social reconstructionist teachings of Brazilian educator Paulo Freire, Aronowitz and Giroux (1985) state that Marxist education theory provides no possibility for counter-hegemonic struggle within schools. They argue that schools as sites of struggle are places where

> particular forms of knowledge, social relations and values can be taught in order to educate students to take their place in society from a position of empowerment rather than from a position of ideological and economic subordination. (Giroux, 1989, p. 115)

The emphasis here would have to be on the phrase, 'can be taught'. The levels of exclusion of, generally, the most vulnerable groups in schools is hardly evidence of students being taught, 'how to take their place in society from a position of empowerment'. In any attempt to empower students, schools face two problems. Firstly, teachers are not taught that schooling is about empowering students, neither are they given adequate preparation through teacher education that would help them support and encourage students to develop their individual identities. How are teachers to develop the identities of their students when they are given so little understanding of diversity and difference in the classroom? Secondly, prescriptive government directives reduce the opportunities for teachers to create environments which are empowering to students. Bottery (1999: 116) argues that

> ...if educationalists have felt over the last few decades that the management, curriculum and ultimate objectives of the system have been drawn more and more into an overarching economic agenda, the signs are that such subordination will intensify. The disappearance of child-centred rhetoric from official publications is plain to see...

These ideas can provide a framework for understanding the rise in exclusions in British schools. They help clarify the way that changes brought about by the 1988 Education Reform Act not only determine the activities of schools but ensure that schools reproduce the inequalities so necessary for maximising economic profitability.

What then are these educational changes which have dictated the activities of schools for more than a decade now?

Education in the market place

The 1988 Education Reform Act has been viewed as a 'process of breaking up the unified education system originally established under the Education Act 1944' (Bridges, 1994: 6). The 1944 Act was, it is argued, an attempt to equalise educational opportunity for children from all classes by placing the responsibility for and supervision of schools within the control of a regional authority. The 1988 Act set about systematically removing this control from the local authority and placing it in the schools themselves. By making funding dependent on schools' abilities to attract students who no longer have to attend schools within their catchment area, and by introducing league tables for examination results, the Act introduced a system of competition which undermined the principles of the Education Act 1944 (Bourne *et al.,* 1994).

Giving schools the responsibility for managing their own financial affairs is also seen as introducing a disincentive to buy in specialist services for children who experience difficulties, thus encouraging schools to exclude rather than help children (Blythe and Milner, 1994). Financial services to schools have in general been reduced, as have the educational resources that schools traditionally depended upon, such as education welfare and psychology services, and specialist learning units (NUT, 1992; Sterling, 1992). In addition, a National Curriculum was introduced despite inadequate consultation with teachers and their unions, and now takes up the bulk of teaching time, 'currently estimated at around 80%' (Gillborn, 1997: 68). It is the examination league tables in particular which are said to have made schools reluctant to admit or retain students who might be seen as having a detrimental effect on their image in relation to both behaviour and performance (Blythe and Milner 1994; Blair, 1994b). The pressure to produce good league table results and the system of teacher appraisal upon which teachers' jobs depend have led to increased pressure on teachers, pressure which places them in a contradictory relationship to their responsibilities to students.

Hargreaves, citing Apple (1988), contends that the intensification of teachers' work had led to a

> reduction of time and opportunity for (elementary) teachers to show care and connectedness to their students because of their scheduled preoccupation with administration and assessment tasks (Hargreaves, 1994:119).

Wexler (1992) argues that the relationship between the teacher and the student is '*the quintessential social relation*', and that for this relationship to work, there must be '*emotional commitment and caring*'. However, 'state-mandated rationalisation of curriculum' has placed strains on this important relationship. In Britain, this rationalisation of curriculum has, through the institution of school league tables, undermined the holistic approach to students' lives that was found to be an important feature of the identities of British teachers. (Broadfoot *et al,* 1988; Nias, 1985). According to Ball (1990), fundamental changes in education have been achieved by means of discourses of derision through which teachers and schools have been presented as not only responsible for the ills of society, but as failing to prepare young people to take up responsible roles in the future. This squeeze on schools, which took place during a time of recession and attempts to regenerate the economy, has worked alongside a more general trend begun by the Conservatives and increasingly realised by the Labour government, to reduce other social services and to create what Elliot Currie (1998) has referred to as the new social Darwinism.

These then are the assumptions of the British school system: that school is a market place, that economic factors are pre-eminent and that children are no longer children but economic units. Governments are then surprised (and of course blame teachers) when students hit back in behaviour terms! Could the expulsion of children from school be part of the contribution that schools are expected to make to economic regeneration? Certainly the Blair government's rhetoric of social inclusion is at odds with these Darwinist trends and it raises the Foucauldian question about 'technologies' of knowledge and power used by the State to control or gain the consent of its citizens.

The next chapter considers how consensus is acquired within the schooling system. I discuss how children and young people are constructed in discourses which help to maintain dominant interests. When teachers are given so little space to think about and question new conventional wisdoms, when they are held to ransom via an appraisal system which measures and rewards their performance along narrow mechanistic lines, the possibilities for challenging the system are reduced and humane faculties such as compassion are dulled or suppressed altogether.

3
Children, schools and the wider society

A dean explained: These kids need to be out. It's unfair to the rest. My job is like a pilot on a hijacked plane. My job is to throw the hijacker overboard'. (Fine, 1991, p.50)

From her study of high-school drop outs in the United States, Fine (*op. cit*) concluded that the high drop out rate in the school she studied was not the result of a conspiracy on the part of the teachers and the school administrators. She states,

> Teachers, administrators, paraprofessionals and aides need only operate as dictated by the state, by history, by tradition, and by the demands of 'efficiency'. As long as they do, often with good intentions and with what they presume to be in the best interests of students, we will continue to witness unequal educational outcomes that correspond, by no means arbitrarily, to the contours of social class, race/ethnicity, gender and disability. (p.26)

What is it, however, which makes teachers and others operate according to the dictates of the state, of history, tradition and 'efficiency', even when this is likely to produce the inequality that teachers claim to work against? The description the dean used of the 'kids' regarded as deviant as highjackers provides an important clue. Becker (1963) states that deviance is a socially attributed label whose application depends on context and on the values of the particular group that defines the behaviour. The highjacker in British schools today is the student who obstructs teachers' attempts to fulfil the new set of criteria as established by the 1988 Education Reform Act, and the demands of the National Curriculum. The infraction of certain school rules now not only carries a higher penalty (exclusion) but requires language that justifies the imposition of this tougher penalty. It is language that attempts to produce consensus on the sanction that is applied. The student who breaks a rule is now, like a highjacker, someone who threatens the safety of others and seeks to destroy their chance to acquire an education and thus reach their destination. This kind of language appeals to new understandings of what education is about, the parameters of which are set by the state, and which teachers are obliged to follow.

The media has played an important role in producing an image of children who are excluded from school as highjackers and who therefore do not conform to normative understandings of what a child should be. Such children, sometimes no older than nine or ten, are presented as 'yobs' (*The Times*, 25 October, 1994; *Daily Mail,* 28 August, 1996) and 'thugs' (*Daily Mirror*, 23 April, 1996), as 'horrors' and 'louts' (*The Sun*, 28 August, 1996) and images of *four year olds* who bite and kick and punch and whom *the teacher is unable to control* (*The Times*, February 15, 1991) violate the public's sense of childhood innocence. Headlines such as 'Is this the worst child in Britain?' (*Guardian*, 23 April, 1996) help to mould public thinking into the view that society is faced with a new breed of child whose roots lie in the 'evil' manifested by the 'freaks of nature' (*Daily Mirror*, 25 November, 1993) – as they called the eleven year old children who killed two-year-old James Bulger.

By accepting these designations, the authoritative and apparently neutral so-called quality newspapers also re-inforce these images. An *Independent* report, for example, saw nothing wrong with a headteacher who admitted that she behaved 'like an ogre' and 'terrified' a four year old in order to teach her to conform (*Independent*, June 15, 1995). The headteacher declared that she 'was an only child *who had never been to playgroup or had any kind of pre-school experience and she had not learned to share*'. She described the behaviour of the child's mother as '*effing and blinding and threatening*', and felt able to tell the mother that she was not surprised that the child could not control her temper, '*if this was the behaviour she saw at home'* (my emphasis). The seemingly neutral presentation of this event and the absence of any sign of disapproval on the part of the reporter would seem to indicate that not only was she in agreement with the headteacher but that she was expecting us, the middle class readers of the *Independent*, to identify instinctively with the headteacher against the mother whom we know *instinctively* to be working class. That we might instead be horrified that a headteacher should find it necessary to 'terrorise' a four year old child is inconceivable in a context where 'they' pose such a threat to the education and well-being of 'our' children.

Politicians too use competitive electoral rhetoric about being 'tough on crime' and talk out of context (as Parsons (1995) observes about Gillian Shepherd and her 'troublesome pupils') adding to public concerns about a degenerating social fabric. The concern to blame parents for this new breed of deviant reverberates in the discourses of exclusion in schools. This process of blaming the parents is by no means new, nor is it confined to Britain (see Haberman, 1995; and Fine, 1991 re the USA). The Scarman Report (1981) on the Brixton disorders of the 1980s was quick to point to parental neglect as a causal factor in the 'moral decadence' of children, whilst the concerns of working class young people (black and white) increasingly finding themselves pushed further and further onto the margins of mainstream society were largely overshadowed (Solomos, 1988). The single parent in particular (usually the mother) is presented in official discourse as the 'demon parent' and invoked to explain many of the ills of society (Ball, 1987). Lone parents and the unemployed are represented in such discourse as scroungers and juxtaposed against the rest of us who are hard-working, tax-paying and therefore responsible citizens. They come to symbolise not the caring society cushioning the most vulnerable, but the nanny state that allows 'us' to be exploited by 'them'. Populist discourse on single parents is used to re-inforce the notion that it is the dysfunctional family which victimises students, who become morally and socially uncontrollable and therefore undeserving of education.

This theme is evident in statements from the teaching unions, which powerfully influence the public perception of students. For example, Nigel de Gruchy, the general secretary of the National Association of Schoolmasters and Union of Women Teachers (NASUWT) presented an image of a beleaguered profession at war with a rising tide of violence in schools, when he stated that

> There is an emerging second generation of violent disrupters whose parents are at the root of the problem (*Independent*, October 11, 1996).

Equally demonising, the Professional Association of Teachers (PAT) called 'for the withdrawal of child benefit from parents who miss Parents' Evenings or fail to ensure that their children attend school' (Searle, 1997:15). Thus the problem of exclusion is defined as a failure of parenting and elides the failure of schools and of the political re-structuring of the education system (Apple, 1990; Ball, 1987).

These examples highlight some of the ways in which the media, teaching unions and politicians mobilise a view of children which 'normalises' public belief in a new generation of 'unchildlike' children who require greater surveillance and greater control for the survival of society. Through these 'truths' about children, both teachers and public appear to lose the instinct for understanding that when, say, four year olds behave in a particular way, they may be trying to communicate a need which they cannot articulate verbally. Studies which contend that a child's future path is set from an early age help to confirm 'our' inability to help 'such' children and influence the disciplinary decisions taken by headteachers in some schools – as I discovered in interview with a certain headteacher. This popular determinist view of children seems to inhibit the ability of adults to think creatively about the needs of little children. As Currie (1998:101) states,

> By itself, the fact that a child's early problems often persists into adolescence may tell us only that no one has seriously tried to deal with them.

Through the 'cultural technologies' (Foucault, 1979) of media, unions and politicians, a consensus can be built around the disciplinary actions of schools. Mass expulsion of children from school becomes a symbol of 'youth in crisis' and of a general moral degeneration in society which justifies teachers' refusal to teach the 'troublemakers' (Searle, 1997). The notion that if the conditions of teachers' lives and work have been made difficult and teachers feel de-skilled and disempowered then this must of necessity impact on students' experience of school, is conveniently buried under the new priorities of the punishment culture.

In the next section I discuss how technologies of representation have been applied to the control of black people with particular reference to black youth, and how these images in turn are harnessed in schools to feed the exclusion process.

Race and ethnicity in schools

A number of studies have attempted to explain the disadvantaged position of black students in the education system in both Britain and the United States. Researchers have sought explanations for lower performance rates of black students in schools and answers have included lower IQ (Eysenck, 1971; Jensen, 1969; Herrnstein and Murray, 1994), differences of culture (Ogbu, 1978; Driver, 1979), low self-esteem (Milner, 1975), poorer behaviour of black students (Ogbu, 1988; Foster, 1990; Hurrell, 1995), resistant youth and peer cultures, (Fordham, 1996; Sewell, 1997;) and the experience of racism and discrimination from teachers and fellow students (Rampton Report, 1981; Swann Report, 1985; Eggleston *et al*, 1986; Mac an Ghaill, 1988; Wright, 1987, 1992b; Brandt, 1990; Gillborn, 1990, 1995a; Mirza, 1992; Troyna and Hatcher, 1992; Troyna, 1993; Wright *et al*, 2000).

The issue of exclusion has newly become a matter for researchers and public debate, although it has always been on the agenda for black communities. In discussions of this problem over the years, it was clear to black communities how greatly the constructed image of the black child had influenced teachers and how this impacted on

31

black students' experience of school. An undated submission by the Camden Community Relations Council (CCRC), to the Rampton Committee, whose report was made public in 1981, stated the following:

> Another practice which is the cause of anxiety and resentment to many West Indian parents and children is that of suspension. It is widely believed that suspension is a device which is too readily used in many schools as a means of dealing with a child who has been labelled 'difficult' or 'disruptive' and that West Indian children are disproportionately represented amongst those to whom the measure is applied. In our view, the hasty categorisation of children as 'difficult' or 'disruptive' often calls in question the capacity of the school staff to understand and provide for the needs of those children. We ask the Rampton Committee to investigate this matter, and to call for an enquiry into the different methods of suspending children used by different authorities and into the 'unofficial' suspensions which occur. The enquiry should elicit information about the numbers of children of different ethnic groups who are suspended. (Para. 8.8)

In 1980, the Inner London Education Authority (ILEA), following the findings by Bernard Coard (1971) that black children were disproportionately represented in disruptive units or 'sin-bins', conducted its own survey of disruptive units. They found that there was an over-representation of minority ethnic group children in all but one of the ILEA divisions (*Issues in Education*, 1981). A study in a West Midlands local authority in 1981 found that teachers' explanations for the disproportionate numbers of minority ethnic group children in disruptive units included a range of pathological explanations such as that black children were 'quick to fly off the handle', or that they were 'more difficult to handle', or that 'West Indian children are lively (sic) and their liveliness gets them into trouble because teachers fear liveliness and schools like silence' (*Educational Issues*, 1981:11). The concentration of so many black children in these units and their designation as emotionally and behaviourally difficult set the tone for future relations between teachers and black students and clearly marked black children as a problem for teachers and for the education system.

The suspension and expulsion of black children from school remained a constant theme at conferences and meetings organised by black communities and in black teachers' associations. The nature of the problem and the level of concern amongst black communities has, moreover, not abated. To talk about the issue of exclusion in school as if it were a recent crisis, as so many media reports have done, is to de-racialise the discussion and distort the facts as they affect a significant number of British students. At least 20 years have passed since the submission by CCRC and almost thirty years since Coard published his findings. Unlike crises which pass, there seems little reason to believe that any strategies taken to deal with the problem of students who are deprived of school will cure the problem of routine exclusion of black and minority children from equal participation in mainstream education. This is a problem which requires a greater understanding of the historical processes which have traditionally affected the education of black and other minority children in school and still continue to do so.

Several writers have argued that black students in both primary and secondary phases of education are disproportionately criticised and apprehended by teachers (Eggleston *et al.* 1986; Mortimore *et al.* 1988; Tizard *et al.* 1988; Mac an Ghaill, 1988; Smith and Tomlinson, 1989; Wright, 1992; Connolly, 1995; Gillborn, 1990; 1995a).

The relationship between white teachers and black students seems, according to Gillborn (1990) to be largely marked by the antagonism frequently generated by teachers. Writing about his study of City College, Gillborn observed that,

> perhaps even more significant than the frequency of criticism and controlling statements which Afro-Caribbean pupils received, was the fact that they were often singled out for criticism even though several pupils of different ethnic origins were engaged in the same behaviour... In sum, Afro-Caribbean pupils were not only criticised more often than their white peers, but the same behaviour in a white pupil might not bring about criticism at all.

Gillborn demonstrated the manner in which this school applied the rules differently to different groups of students. He divided the rules of the school into those which were 'routine' or commonly under-stood, and those which were 'interpretive'. The interpretive rules were those which were not clearly defined but 'related to less explicit expectations of acceptable behaviour'. He wrote

> In comparison to white and Asian pupils therefore, a greater pro-portion of detentions given to Afro-Caribbean pupils appear to have been based upon offences whose identification rested primarily in the *teacher's interpretation* (my emphasis) of pupil attitude or intention (p.40).

Given this situation it is perhaps unsurprising that so many studies have pointed to conflict between teachers and black students, and to this being a major cause leading up to exclusion (Stirling, 1993; Sewell, 1997; Wright *et al.*, 2000).

Others have pointed not only to the differential treatment of black students within British schools but to the often inadequate or in-appropriate and sometimes reluctant policy responses to these ex-periences (Troyna, 1992; 1993; Gillborn, 1995b).

In order to understand how the 'inner eye' transmits commonsense racism, it is necessary to understand the ways in which race has been constructed in Britain. I present only a brief overview of literature which helps to clarify the salience of race and racialised processes and procedures in the British context.

Racialising Education

Foucault (1979) refers to 'regimes of truth' which are constructions of reality in ways which the public can assimilate and accept. The creation of such regimes of truth around race is by no means a new phenomenon. From early representations of white Europeans as 'normal', it was an easy step to the construction of black people as the 'abnormal Other' (Curtin, 1968; Jordan, 1968; Fanon, 1970; Rattansi and Donald, 1992; Delgado and Stefanic, 1997). Rattansi and Donald describe an historical link between the British encounter with black people and the position of 'the lower classes' within Britain itself, arguing that there was always a relationship between race and class in this encounter with the Other. The presence of these

Others in visible numbers in British schools presented a particular threat which led in the 1960s and 1970s to the system of dispersal (bussing of minority group children in order to ensure that they constituted less than 30% in any one school)[6]. On the one hand, there was the historical legacy of an education system which utilised a deficit model of working class children and the children of the poor in determining what kind of education to provide for the masses. On the other hand, there was the racist legacy of a former colonial government which feared that standards in the schools would be lowered and the education of white children would be affected. This view of black children, mainly of Caribbean origin, led to many of them being placed in disruptive units or sin-bins in numbers disproportionate to their presence in schools (Coard, 1971).

This centuries-old image of black people as educationally inferior and behaviourally dangerous continues, moreover, to be reproduced through the educational discourse of under-achievement (Troyna, 1988), and now through exclusions. Troyna argued that rather than provoking questions about the education of black children, under-achievement has become part of the received wisdom about the essential ineducability of black students, and the stereotype of the hardworking Asian student has often, as Tomlinson (1984) says, been used as 'a stick with which to beat the West Indian'. In other words, in addition to the image that blackness itself conjures up, terms such as underachievement and disruptive have helped to normalise teachers' perception of black students.

The Problem of Black Youth

It is, however, adolescents, and more precisely black male youth, that seem to represent the enemy within, around whom moral panics have been constructed in the everyday discourses of schools. Hall *et al.* (1978:16) define a moral panic as occuring

> when the official reaction to a person, groups of persons or series of events is out of all proportion to the actual threat posed.

To judge from the excessive over-representation of black students amongst those excluded from school, black young people, and in

35

particular black males, must indeed be seen to pose an overwhelming threat to the order of schools. We know, for example, that black boys are seven to eight times more likely to be excluded from school than white boys, and between four to six times more likely to be excluded than black girls (SEU, 1998; Wright *et. al*. 2000). This image, however, must not be allowed to obscure the difficulties and problems faced by black girls in the education system (Brah and Minhas, 1985; Mac an Ghaill, 1988; Mirza, 1992; Noguera, 1997). Mirza, for example, describes the subtle and not so subtle ways in which black girls were marginalized and excluded in the school she studied, whilst Noguera, describing the African-American experience, warns against a singular focus on black males which can lead to absolutist solutions which not only ignore the needs and concerns of black females, but are themselves in danger of re-inforcing the idea that black males are fundamentally deficient in some way. Black women have been the subject of different kinds of representation which have assisted different forms of oppression both in the wider society (Gilman, 1992) and in the private or domestic sphere. Without losing sight of the invisible hand which controls black girls and of the multivalence of the black experience, it is nevertheless necessary to trace the genealogy of black males in Britain in order to understand the contribution that a racialised, classed and gendered framework might have on the disproportionate numbers of black boys amongst those suspended and expelled from school.

Negative representations of black youth (read male) as a group threatening the social order of Britain began in the 1970s, when the first substantial number of young black people born in Britain began to assert themselves and refused to accept the assimilationist tendencies of their parents. But these representations had their roots deeper in history, as discussed above (Rattansi and Donald, 1992). Although the image of black children as disruptive began when the 70s generation was in the primary school (via their mass allocation to sin-bins), the urban disturbances of the 1980s seemed to fix in the minds of white society the image of young black men as representing trouble. The race riots of white people which took place over the middle of the last century in Liverpool, London and

Nottingham, were themselves presented as a problem of an 'alien' presence destroying the British 'idyll' (Solomos, 1988). It was an easy shift in the 1980s to the construction of black young people as representative of a lawless culture which was both threatening and un-British. The public belief that Britain is naturally a peaceful and law-abiding country projected an image of crime and disorder as being an alien or foreign disease, and men as particular carriers of the more violent manifestation of this disease (Pearson, 1983). In the 1970s and 1980s, a **Black Youth** identity was being constructed via media discourses of 'blacks' whose 'unpredictable' and 'volatile' nature was apt to erupt into 'race riots' (Solomos, 1988); as 'muggers' (Hall *et. al*, 1978), preying, as Enoch Powell saw it, on helpless old ladies; re-inforced in academic studies as having 'a penchant for violence' (cf.Cashmore and Troyna, 1982) and realised through police harassment which became part of the routine experience, especially of black men, into the 1990s (Gilroy, 1987; Gordon, 1988; CRE, 1997).

This overwhelming assault on the identities of black young people was met with different kinds of resistance, not least of which was that black young people turned to religion in the form of the Rastafarian faith (Small, 1983). Professor Stuart Hall of the Open University declared in a television interview that, '*that generation (of the 1970s) would have committed a social collective suicide if they had not had that kind of black identity*'. In the same television programme, Lee Jasper of the Society of Black Lawyers declared that education during that time was something on which he looked back with anger. '*It was a waste of a whole community*', he said (BBC2, Empire Windrush Series, 13 June, 1998).

The 1990s saw no release from this kind of assault on young black people. In 1995, Sir Paul Condon, the Metropolitan Commissioner of Police, revived the image of the black mugger, thus re-inforcing the essential **criminality** of black people and particularly black men in the social psyche. The representation of black men as having particular tendencies, or drives and inclinations has thus justified their closer surveillance by the police and in school; has justified

37

their exclusion from school and their constant presence before the criminal justice system (Scraton *et al*, 1991). It is not the crime, but the criminality that has been the focus of attention. It fed in teachers what Gillborn has described as 'the myth of the Afro-Caribbean challenge', which was the widespread belief that 'both as individuals and as a group, Afro-Caribbean pupils were especially prone to threatening teachers' authority'(1990:57).

The myth operated in such a way that, as Gillborn continues, 'any offence by an Afro-Caribbean pupil could be interpreted as indicative of a more general 'attitude' (an inner drive)' (*op.cit.* p.59).

However, the concern to represent black youth as a criminal element and a threat is not only a racialised discourse but articulates also with a wider ideological project to represent 'truths' about the poor, the homeless and the dispossessed as objects to be feared, despised, and locked away (Cavadino and Dignan, 1997; Worrall, 1997; Goldberg and Evans, 1998; Stern, 1998; Currie, 1998). The participation of schools in this punishment culture has clear implications for the human rights of students, as I discuss in the next section.

Schools and the creation of criminals

According to the National Association for the Care and Rehabilitation of Offenders (NACRO) 'Research and experience have long suggested that those who fare badly at school are more at risk of becoming offenders than those who do well' (1998, p.3).

In their report, *Children, Schools and Crime* (1998) NACRO reported the following:

> According to the 1991 National Prison Survey, almost half of prisoners said that they had left school before the age of 16, compared to 11% of the general population. 1% of prisoners said that they had never been to school and almost half had problems with literacy and numeracy. More recent studies of young people in young offender institutions (YOIs) have found very high rates of educational failure. The Chief Inspector of Prison's 1997 review of 'Young Prisoners' found that most 'had been failed by the education system'. More recently, the Basic Skills Agency conducted in-depth interviews with

500 offenders aged 17-20 serving custodial sentences and found that 21% could not write their name and address without error, half had difficulty telling the time and the days of the week in the right order, and fewer than a third could fill in a job application form satisfactorily (p.3).

Similar reports come from the USA. The US Department of Justice National Institute of Corrections Centre in Washington DC gives information about a survey of inmates carried out in Illinois prisons which asked prisoners about their educational background. They found that 72% of inmates interviewed were high-school drop-outs (Jones and Myrant, 1991 p.203).

NACRO established four key links between schooling and crime. These were anti-social and criminal behaviour within schools, low achievement, absenteeism and suspensions and expulsions. They wrote:

...there appears to be an even stronger link between children who are suspended, expelled or excluded from school and their propensity to offend. In the Home Office Study, a high proportion of those who had been temporarily excluded were offenders. As for children who had been permanently excluded, though absolute numbers in the study were small, the link was very strong. All eleven of the permanently ex-cluded boys were offenders. The Audit Commission's report, 'Misspent Youth', found that almost two-thirds of children appearing in court had also been excluded from school or were regular truants (p.5).

The human rights implications of school disciplinary exclusions are clearly profound. Should students really bear the full brunt of the problems created by the inability of schools to properly define their purpose, and of the problems created for teachers by government ideologies? What are some of the implications of placing young people in a position where they become vulnerable to involvement in the criminal justice system? How is society to deal with this in-creasing number of offenders?

A number of commentators in the US are beginning to link the growing divide between rich and poor with the growth and privatisa-tion of prisons, as well as the increasing use of prisons as industrial complexes. The prison industry has been described as one of the twenty fastest growing industries in the United States, only slightly behind data processing and computer software (Beckett, 1997). Goldberg and Evans (1998) see the introduction of 'three strikes' and of mandatory minimum sentences as a cynical ploy to ensure that the prison population will continue to grow. There are other sinister aspects to this growth. Tonry (1995) records that incarceration rates in the USA are seven times higher for black people than they are for whites. It is estimated that 'at the current rate of incarceration, by 2010, the majority of all African-American men between the ages of 18 and 40 will be in prison' Hanrahan, (1998:33).

The signs that Britain is increasingly going in the same direction are quite obvious, regardless of the 'social inclusion' rhetoric of the Government. According to Scraton *et al.* (1991), the UK is second only to Luxemburg in relation to rates of incarceration in Europe, and this has been supported by a rapid expansion of the prison building programme. Sir Steven Tumim (1997) agrees, stating that the rate of imprisonment in Britain is higher than almost anywhere else in Western Europe. Worrall (1997) cites Gardiner (1995) as arguing that the 1991 Criminal Justice Act in Britain targets the 'underclass', that is, whole communities, rather than individuals. Tumim (*op.cit.*) suggests that as the poor get poorer and more people become poor, there will also be more crime and greater need to find ways of containing it. He expresses a hope for an expansion of the *industrial* prison in Britain. He hopes this expansion will be a means of improving the sense of usefulness of the prisoner and also the ability to prepare prisoners for life outside. For all its good intentions, this view is based on a fundamental belief in the justice of the British penal system. Yet during his round of inspections Sir Stephen could hardly have failed to notice the over-representation of black men and women in British prisons. His belief that the poor commit more crime because they are poor is not a sufficient explanation for this over-representation. Black people, who account for just over 1% of the population, comprise, according to Cavadino and Dignan (1997), 11% of the male and 20% of the female prison population. They state:

it is estimated that on current (British) trends, nearly one in 10 young black men will have received a custodial sentence before his 21st birthday, double the proportion of their white peers (p.274).

They also note that there is no evidence that black people commit more crime than other groups, whereas there is abundant evidence that black people experience differential treatment within the criminal justice system (see also Scraton *et al*, 1991 and Worral, 1997).

Alarmist though the above account sounds, it helps to underline the human rights implications of expelling young people from school. Could the unacceptably high level of black students who ,are excluded from school indeed lead to a 'social collective suicide' as they are further and further excluded and alienated from society? How much thought is given to the future of the individual when the school decides to expel a student? To what extent are the demands made on schools and teachers considered as contributory factors when making what could be a disastrously life-changing decision for the student?

This chapter has outlined the contradictory position of schools in relation to the exclusion (in both a disciplinary and a 'routine' sense) of students. It focused on forms of representation of children which help to justify such action. I have also argued that black children and their communities have a particular relationship with the education system and it is only by understanding the historical development of this relationship that we can understand the *over-representation* of black students in exclusions. Negative constructions of children, and of black children in particular, provide teachers with a 'handle' for understanding and making sense of the behaviours of certain categories of students. These constructions are tools for building consensus on what schools are about and provide teachers and administrators in schools with the rationale for exclusion. In the following chapters, I explore the role of headteachers and teachers in the exclusion process and ask what room there is for agency, for the individual as well as for the school as whole, to make decisions that do not adversely affect the lives of young people.

Note

6. The system of 'bussing' children in Britain and that which happened in the USA in the 1960s had very different histories and causes. In the USA it was part of an attempt to end segregation in schools. In Britain, it was a response to large numbers of new immigrants arriving in Britain, many of whom were located in the same areas and so whose children attended the same schools. This was believed to lead to a lowering of standards for the white children in these schools.

4
Leadership and disciplinary exclusion

Many studies have investigated the issue of leadership in schools. They invariably conclude that the role of the headteacher is significant in influencing the type of culture or ethos of the school (Jones, 1987; Blase and Anderson, 1995; Grace, 1995) and in helping to shape the experiences of both learners and teachers (Blase and Blase, 1994). Studies have also noted the demanding and conflicting role of the headteacher as she or he is made accountable for 'a complex, ill-defined and unbiddable set of variables, each of which may appear to make equal and opposite demands' (Jones, 1987:6).

The headteacher's role is made particularly difficult during times of radical educational change, especially change that is imposed from 'above', with little if any consultation with those upon whom these new demands are made (Grace, 1995). Grace asserts that the market priorities imposed on schools have had profound implications for school leadership as 'moral relations and professional relations are giving ground before the rise of market relations in education' (p.41).

Grace views this displacement of the moral and interpersonal caring aspects of schooling as placing headteachers in a particularly difficult situation in relation to school exclusions. He observes that in his study,

> Headteachers found themselves attempting to balance the individual care and welfare of particular pupils with considerations of the

general welfare of the majority of the pupils. This dilemma was compounded by the headteachers' understanding that their classroom teachers expected 'strong leadership' about, and 'protection' from disruptive and challenging pupils. At an implicit level, headteachers were aware that their colleagues expected them 'to deal with', 'get rid of' or otherwise resolve problems related to disruptive pupils. (p.152)

Jones (1987:7), on the other hand, asserts that

Very few heads have been selected for their qualities of leadership in troubled times, their ability to resolve conflict or to straddle uncomfortable polarities, nor, by and large, have they been trained in these skills, even though training is possible.

Equally worrying is the absence of leadership training for headteachers to lead in an educational context which has become much more complex with the incorporation in British schools of so many different cultures, religions and languages. Not only are headteachers in multi-ethnic contexts expected to steer their schools up the ladder of academic success as measured by their position in the school league tables, but they are also expected to resolve religious, political and ethnic conflicts which even politicians might find difficult to understand, let alone resolve.

But other important questions about headteachers' personal values regarding children and young people need to be addressed in training. Should a headteacher actually like children and have a sense of *compassion* for and *commitment* to them in order to take a holistic approach to their needs? Should a headteacher *understand* children and young people so they can foster an ethos where they are treated as people and respected as beings with feelings and a sense of their own identity? Should a headteacher have the skills to *enable* staff to empower children and young people and the *humility* to learn from staff whose skills with students are recognised? Should a headteacher have the *wisdom* to recognise that teachers and other members of non-teaching staff are human, and that compassion is due to them as much as it is to students? Do headteachers acknowledge that staff have different starting points in their understanding of controversial issues and that what they need is to be given strength and encouragement to *want* to learn and understand these issues? Should a headteacher have the *courage* to make difficult and sometimes contentious decisions even in the face of opposition?

The general thrust of this chapter is to argue that individual headteachers can make disciplinary choices (however limited and however constrained) which can make the difference between destroying a student's future and giving that student a chance to become an accepted and productive citizen. The characteristics outlined above are particularly salient in relation to issues of discipline. The headteacher's starting point is important. Headteachers might approach discipline from the standpoint that it is about punishment and not about teaching better behaviour. They might regard students who break rules as 'yobs' or 'thugs' who should not be in school at all, let alone 'my' school. It could be that they believe some students are vulnerable through no fault of their own, but that the school is not a welfare service and therefore cannot deal with 'students with problems'. On the other hand, they could take the view that these vulnerable students need more understanding and caring than the average student, meaning that more thoughtful ways of dealing with them will be required. The starting point could be an understanding that some students may be provoked and respond or retaliate in ways that are unacceptable – as is often the case with one-off offences – but that, with education and caring, they are redeemable.

It is recognised that the challenge for headteachers in multi-ethnic schools is great, given the notions about race and education discussed earlier. They may well face greater pressure from teachers to exclude black students for reasons which are largely based on, or are the consequence of, stereotypes and assumptions about race and ethnicity. The type of leadership offered by the headteacher, and the kind of culture or ethos which prevails in the school is therefore crucial to the fate of its students (Wright *et.al.* 2000). I suggest that this culture or ethos depends in large part on headteachers' own values and beliefs, and on their orientation towards or away from punishment as the means for resolving student misdemeanours. Next, I examine each of the qualities and values mentioned above and, using examples, consider whether headteachers do indeed have agency and whether they can make a difference to the lives of usually the most vulnerable students in their schools.

Compassion and commitment

In considering these values, I look at the ideological orientation of the headteacher in relation to whether she or he takes a traditional punishment view of disciplining students, or whether s/he is able to adopt a more personal approach which takes as its starting point the education of the offending student. I provide examples to show that choices are available to headteachers and that the decisions they make have significant impact – either positive or negative – on their students.

Ms Christian (the names of all schools and people in the studies have been changed) is the Head of Catholic High School with a population of 700 students. It is a multi-ethnic school with approximately 30% black students, 3% students of South Asian origin (Bangladesh, India and Pakistan), and about 1% refugee and 'Other' students. The rest of the student body, approximately 64%, are white and mainly of Irish origin. The students attending the school are drawn from a wide catchment area of Catholic primary schools. The general profile of students is working class, with substantial numbers from all ethnic groups receiving free school meals. The school is situated in a poor area of a large city. This area has all the hallmarks of deprivation, such as poverty, poor housing, crime, and high levels of unemployment, especially of black people. Most of the black students live in this area. At the time I visited the school, Ms Christian had not permanently excluded a student in three years and the general thrust was to keep students in school if at all possible.

Aurin was a student at Catholic High School – a fifteen year old Year 10 Irish boy with a 'very troubled background'. Staff in the school had reached the point where they felt they could no longer teach him. He truanted more than he attended, and when he did attend, he made life impossible for the teachers and other students. The point had arrived when teachers were no longer prepared to have him in their classrooms. Ms Christian had a meeting with her staff to discuss the student. They had worked with other services such as social services and education welfare to try to keep Aurin in school, but this had not helped. It was time to consider removing him from the school.

However, Ms Christian had concluded that basically Aurin was not a bad sort and that to remove him from school would simply ensure that he ended up in the same place as his parents – in prison. So she asked the staff whether they would give him one more chance by helping him work on a special programme which might help him gain some academic qualifications. He had fallen so far behind the syllabus that there was little chance of his gaining any passes. He was allowed to drop four of his subjects and concentrate on the five he enjoyed most (including English and Maths). The headteacher showed a personal interest in him, talking to him about his future ambitions and about how he might best achieve them. As he was a particularly difficult case, she decided to mentor him personally. She talked to him about his interests, his life, and told him that he could talk to her about any difficulties he might be facing, whether at home or in school. He sat in a room near her office when his subjects were not being taught, and did his homework or worked on what he had already missed. The Head warned him that his future was in his own hands, but that the staff were willing to work with him to help him achieve his goals. He had to attend school, he had to catch up with his subjects, he had to co-operate with the staff, who would do all they could to help him. When he felt particularly troubled, there was someone he could talk to. Aurin managed an attendance record of 97% and obtained his General Certificate of Secondary Education (GCSEs). Ms Christian told me that

> He was beaming like an infant when I told him that he had achieved 97% attendance. He had made it his business to be in school and do the GCSEs he could. ...He has turned out to be a lad you can talk to and he has his GCSEs! (Blair and Bourne 1998, p.196)

What is obvious here is the compassion with which this headteacher viewed the student's problems. Aurin's difficult family circumstances were recognised, but rather than expel him for the psychological effects his personal problems created, the school decided that he needed protecting and he needed help.

Was it the Catholic ethos or mission statement which made this possible? As it was not the local environment or the socio-economic circumstances of the students, could it have been the size of the school? These factors were not what determined the outcome for this student. It was the personal sense of compassion and caring exhibited by the headteacher and encouraged in her staff. The evidence can be found by comparing Ms Christian with the headteachers of two other Catholic schools, both of them similar to Ms Christian's in terms of size and the socio-economic profiles of the students. Indeed Ms Christian's students were drawn from an area which was much more disadvantaged than was the case for the other schools. The headteacher of one of the other schools regarded students who did not conform as 'hijackers' and expelled students without much ado. The other was more compassionate in his approach and preferred not to expel students, but he felt unable to go against the wishes of his staff.

Another teacher, Mr Friend, had a different orientation towards the exclusion of students. He is the headteacher of a large multi-ethnic comprehensive, a split-site school with approximately 600 students on each site. Deputy Heads take overall charge of each section, but decisions about disciplinary exclusions are taken by Mr Friend. I provide here details of an Exclusion Hearing in order to illustrate the headteacher's personal orientation and the results this produces for students.

The hearing

My attendance at this meeting was cleared with the student and his mother and with the school governors. Present at the meeting were the student, his mother, the headteacher, school administrator, five governors and a representative from the Local Education Authority.

The hearing took place in the headteacher's office. I was not allowed to tape-record the meeting but was permitted to take detailed notes of the proceedings. This was easily achieved as I was not allowed to say anything and did not have to interact with the participants.

The boy, Luigi, was of part Italian and part Bangladeshi origin. He was fourteen years old and in his third year. He was being expelled for bringing an airgun to school and compounded his offence by loading it and handing it to another boy. Thus he created a dangerous situation not only for himself but for other students too. Luigi's explanation was that he had found the gun and had decided to take it in order to protect himself against threats by white youths on his council estate who sometimes followed him shouting racial abuse and had threatened to 'cut his face'. He had taken the airgun out of his bag in the toilets to show to another boy. He admitted that it had been a 'stupid thing to do' and said he was sorry. Mr Friend, however, revealed that not only had Luigi taken the gun out of his bag, he had also threatened to beat up another boy if he told anyone that he had witnessed Luigi's actions. After Mr Friend had outlined the case against the student and Luigi had explained his actions to the panel, the meeting proceeded as follows:

> **Mr Friend**: We are not trying to be punitive but protective. Luigi needs help. He has experienced traumas in his life which have not necessarily led to the event but may have contributed to it. He has problems which are not of his own making. He has been having trouble with the Dew Street gang. The Asians are being picked on and they are beginning to fight back. But we cannot allow sympathy for the boy to overrule the bigger issue of the welfare of the students.

> **Chair of Governors**: But is this incident sufficient? He has not been excluded before.

> **Mr Friend**: What it does is give an indication of how his mind works. He is dangerous. He brought an airgun to school knowing its danger, he loaded it, and he handed it to someone else. It is the conscious, premeditated nature of the action.

> **Governor**: How did his threats to the other boy come to light?

Mr Friend: There is a rule that children have to report anything dangerous. It was the boy who was threatened with violence who told. But Luigi knew how the gun worked with precision, and yet he still brought it into school against the strongest prohibition. Luigi is too dangerous to have in the school. He has risked the lives of others.

Mother: But he disagrees with what you say happened. He is not dangerous. This is the first time that something like this has happened. He has never been dangerous. There have been no complaints about violence. He is being judged wrongly. There are two gangs on the estate. He needs protection.

Mr Friend: I am shocked about the gangs. I've asked the police and they have confirmed that there is a lot of aggression of young people on the estate. But my task as the Head is not to put moral blame. Luigi needs help to be able to handle such situations with discussion. He needs *official* help (my emphasis).

Mother: But he was not given the opportunity to explain himself.

Chair of Governors: What were you intending to do with the gun?

Luigi: Only to threaten (the racist gangs), not to use it. I wouldn't have the bottle to use it. I loaded it because Scot wanted to know how it's done. I only told Eric that I would boot him because I was reacting to his provocation. I didn't say that I would beat him up. It's not the first time that he has annoyed me around the school.

Chair of Governors (addressing the Head): Is it your wish that he be excluded for the rest of the year and rejoin in September?

Mother: He could go to counselling until September. I could work at him while he is being counselled.

Mr Friend: According to the 1944 Act, Mrs M. has a duty to educate her child in the best way she can. There is no specific need for this to be an exclusion, but whether he would have the right to return in September would depend on whether or not he has been judged to be dangerous.

Governor: If Luigi were excluded, Mrs M. would still have the right to re-apply in September.

LEA officer: As he is a resident of this borough, the LEA would have to take responsibility....

After some discussion of the mechanisms for allowing the boy back into the school after a temporary period out, Mr Friend, Mrs M. (Luigi's mother), Luigi and I leave the room while the governors make their decision. When we are called back in, it is to hear the following verdict.

> **Chair of Governors:** We have decided to uphold Mr Friend's decision to exclude permanently. We cannot allow gang warfare in the school. We have a responsibility to the other students. We believe that Luigi has contravened the school rules to an unacceptable extent......

Throughout the proceedings, I was forcibly struck by one fact – the unequal power relations of that situation. The meeting was held in Mr Friend's office, not in a neutral space. Mr Friend sat upright, presenting his case against the child in an articulate and confident manner. He dominated the whole discussion, invoking his professional duty to all his students while also quoting his responsibilities under the law. He was addressing his peers in a language with which they were able to engage and which held their attention and commanded respect. Mrs M., on the other hand, sat with her body hunched forward, and her fingers constantly twisting the strap of the handbag on her lap. She seemed nervous and spoke hesitatingly with a strong London accent. She said very little throughout. Luigi was more articulate than his mother, but apart from his initial explanation and the one question addressed to him, he and his mother were not given the same opportunity as the headteacher to present their case to the panel. There was no follow-up of her insistence that the facts may not have been as the headteacher presented them. I later wrote in my diary that 'The mother didn't stand a chance. There were eight authority figures in judgement of the boy. It was like a court case in which there were several prosecutors and no-one for the defence'.

It was also interesting to see how the Governors interpreted the events. Their conclusion was that what Luigi had done was to introduce gang warfare into the school, whereas the only gang warfare alluded to in the case was that between different ethnic groups on the council estate, and *not* in the school. Luigi had taken the gun in order to protect himself from racist groups who taunted him on the way to school but were not themselves students of the school. His actual offence was to bring the gun into school and to demonstrate to a friend how it was loaded.

The argument here is not about condoning such dangerous activities by students. It is right and proper that schools should have rules which protect all members of the institution and something needs to be done when students breach these rules. The choice the head-teacher had in this case was either to interpret the student's action as a deep-seated psychological problem, or, despite the dangerous nature of the incident, to interpret it as a childish prank which, with proper education and counselling, would not be repeated. The student did not, after all, have a record of bad behaviour in the school. In fact two of his teachers with whom I discussed the ex-clusion were dismayed at the decision taken by the governors, one of them describing Luigi as 'a decent lad'. During the Hearing, one of the governors questions the severity of the headteacher's decision, given that the student had not been excluded before. For Mr Friend, it is the apparently premeditated nature of the action that points to a psychological inclination to dangerous behaviour on the part of the student. However, pleas by the mother that her son be given time out of school in order to receive counselling is met without a response. When it is suggested that the student could return again in the new academic year, Mr Friend's reply is to invoke the 1944 Education Act which places responsibility on the parent, and not the school, to ensure that the child receives an education. This seems to indicate that Mr Friend had decided not to have the student in his school, whatever the arguments. It is difficult to see how, in this case, the headteacher could have argued that permanent exclusion was, for him, 'a last resort'.

Understanding students

By 'understanding' I mean dealing with students in a manner that is responsive to their age, gender, ethnicity, religion as well as their individual circumstances. The headteacher who terrorised a four year old seems to me to have little understanding of children. How many parents would trust such a person with their infants? Could the mother of the child be blamed for 'effing and blinding' as was reportedly her response to her child's treatment? Understanding is required right across all phases. The emerging adolescent, for example, requires a particular kind of understanding.

A number of writers who have studied this age group contend that schools do not seem to understand and therefore cannot effectively support the emotional development of adolescents (Curtis and Bidwell, 1977; Mickelson, 1990; Gottfredson *et.al.*1993; Hargreaves *et al,* 1996; Cullingford and Morrison, 1997). These writers argue that there seems to be little understanding of the complex process of acquiring independence which is a part of growing up. For adolescents in Western societies, acquiring independence necessarily involves a period of contrariness as they try to resolve the conflict between attempts to please both the adults from whom they are trying to break away and the peer group from whom they have their identities affirmed. Curtis and Bidwell (1977,p.46) go so far as to state that

> The adult must (expect) rudeness or even insults from the emerging adolescent who is struggling for independence. It is not intended that rudeness be condoned by the teacher without comment, nor is docile acceptance recommended. The need is for teachers and staff to see these behaviours for what they are, a striving of the youngster for a meaningful relationship both within himself (sic) and with others. Pupils must learn that rudeness is not the correct method of expression, *but they will not learn this if they are faced with similar rude and punitive expressions from staff* (my emphasis). Acceptance of the person and the need for expression without approval of the specific rude behaviour is a recommended procedure.

Hargreaves *et.al* (1996:31) talk about the need adolescents have to feel that teachers care for them. Adolescence, they state, '*is a time for establishing and testing perceptions of self as worthwhile individuals*'. Teachers are 'significant others' to whom young people look for confirmation of their acceptance and status as people who matter.

In a survey I carried out of 200 Year 10 students in one secondary school, the majority of students felt that teachers spoke to them rudely and showed them little respect. They particularly resented it when teachers shouted at or humiliated them, especially in the presence of others. Students said things like:

'Their body language. It's just rude. And the way they talk to you, man, it's just so rude'.

'It's the tone of voice which they use in front of the whole class'

'Say you're talking, yeah, and they say things like, 'shut up''.

But even where a teacher was guilty of instigating an incident, students felt that the headteacher would take the side of the teacher against the student. This seems to be quite common in cases where students report teacher racism. In one situation, a headteacher told me that he was incensed when a student accused one of the teachers of racism. He immediately took the student's records out and pointed out to him the extent of his misdemeanours in the school. Under the circumstances, he said, he considered the student's accusation to be a case of 'reverse racism'. This brings to mind the discussion about motive raised in chapter 1. The headteacher clearly did not believe that the teacher had been racist. This was a colleague whom he knew to be professional in her work. Such a person, he believed, could never be racist. The student's experience was dismissed, and he was not only considered to be himself a racist, but the record of his poor behaviour was considered evidence that this was so. It came as no surprise to me when this student was excluded. No effort had been made to understand him, either as a young person or as a black person. His own record of bad behaviour meant to this headteacher that he was not deserving of a hearing, nor deserving of understanding. But why would he have interpreted the teacher's behaviour as racist? Was there something to be learnt from this student's experience which might have helped clarify why students make these accusations of racism?

When students feel that they have a strong and legitimate complaint to make but feel unsupported by the Head, this sets up a culture of

'Them' and 'Us' in the school. In one school, there was a strong policy of inclusiveness where everyone worked towards building in students a sense of community and identity with the school. There was a strong 'We' culture and students felt that the staff in the school led by example in the way they treated the students, whatever their ethnicity. Students were never shouted at or humiliated, their concerns were listened to and taken seriously. From this they learnt to respect themselves, their fellow students and the teachers.

Understanding black students

Stereotypes prevent proper understanding of black students. One student told me:

> With white teachers, when new black kids come to the school, they just think they are going to turn out to be thugs anyway so they might as well treat them with disrespect... So even if you are not doing anything bad, like say you are borrowing a ruler, they want to get under your nerves, so they twist the situation to make it look like you are doing something wrong.

The concern here, as so often when black students accuse white teachers of racism, is not *necessarily* whether or not this is true. The vital question is: what has happened to make black students arrive at this conclusion and experience their interactions with teachers in this negative way? This is the question schools need to engage with in order to understand and respond appropriately to black students. The position taken by the Head, who is ultimately responsible for setting the tone and the direction the school will take, is crucial.

Ms Christian was conscious of the need to listen closely to students and try to grasp their points of view. She was sensitive to the fact that, as a white woman, she needed to try especially hard to understand the experience and world views of black students and their families. She did this first of all by approaching students with an open mind about their experience. She was willing to believe them, knowing that their experience was not her experience – so who was she to say they were not telling the truth? When students talked about racism, Ms Christian realised that she had not fully grasped the nature of the experience black students brought with them to school and the extent to which this experience was perpetuated in the school. She needed to engage with their concerns and create an environment in which black students did not have to carry grievances around with them. The grievance was based not only on the trigger incident in school but also on experiences outside of school such as police harassment, and a long memory which went beyond that generation of students. She therefore knew that she had to make it her business to understand about the lives of her students both inside and outside school. She initiated discussions with the staff about how best to respond to the needs of black students. It was important for this not to be – and especially for black students not to see it as – a token exercise, designed to control them and secure their compliance. This consultation exercise led to actual policy decisions and to changes in the very culture of the school in relation to how racism was dealt with. The result was an environment in which black students felt able to trust the Head and the teachers. One student in the school summed it up:

> If something like this happens, (unfair treatment of a black student) or you are unhappy with a particular teacher, you can go and see the Head or the Deputy Head, because we have a Code of Conduct in the school which says what the procedures are.

Enabling

An enabling headteacher is one who observes closely what each member of staff in the school experiences (Greenfield, 1991) and what each has to offer. The headteacher's central motivation must be the interests of the students, because, as Greenfield argues, it is this which '(shapes) the principal's orientation to teachers and, in turn, her capacity to influence teachers to adopt certain goals or pursue certain lines of action' (p.172). Some headteachers see themselves as team workers, sharing the leadership of the school with the staff, and are open-minded about ideas which promote the best interests of the students. Such headteachers recognise and learn from the different skills their staff bring to the school. Some members of staff are highly regarded by students and some seem to develop a particular empathy with black students. The focus is first and foremost on the students.

Three headteachers stand out in my studies as good examples of this – Ms Quashie, Head of a primary school which did not exclude children (LEA study), Ms Christian, the Head of Catholic School, and Ms Daniel, the Head of a Boys' Comprehensive school (DfEE study). These headteachers consulted with and took advice from staff members. The two white headteachers, Ms Daniel and Ms Christian, were not afraid to seek help and advice from black communities and from those working in the field of race and ethnicity. But they also went further and organised staff in-service education on these issues. Ms Christian in particular was pro-active about incorporating issues of equity and equality into school policy.

Other headteachers might see themselves as the captains of the ship: they determine the route, make the decisions, give the orders, and basically lead from as far in front as possible. The market culture into which schools have been thrust seems to have pushed many headteachers into this style of leadership. The focus of these headteachers will essentially be the efficient functioning of the institutions they lead. It is a leadership style which, as I have already discussed, is less empathetic to the needs of students in general (Grace, 1995; Postman, 1996), and in some ways, for example in the area of discipline, hostile to the needs of black students (Wright et.al., 2000). What seems to have happened as a result of turning schools into markets at the expense of the development of young people is that the teaching of morals, of sharing and community no longer seem to be considered a part of the school's role. The focus is on punishing students for not sharing, or for using violence or breaking some other rule, rather than on educating them about constructive ways of negotiating one's path through life. Yet in all the studies on which this book is based, students complain that rules are inconsistently implemented or punishment unfairly given. Students felt that not only did rules operate unfairly against them but that teachers were often themselves guilty of instigating an incident for which a student was punished. Lawrence (15 years old) says:

> I was standing in the corridor and the teacher bumped into me and then very rudely told me to get out of the way. I thought, 'He bumps into me, no apology, and then roughly tells me to get out of the way'. So I said to him, 'First of all you walk into me and then you start ordering me about trying to make me look bad in front of everyone when you were the one in the wrong'. In the end it turned into a big thing and I was excluded.

This teacher may have been exceptional or this kind of behaviour may be more common in schools where stress levels are high. Either way, rudeness to students is a self-defeating exercise which in turn generates rudeness from students. To quote Curtis and Bidwell (1977) again, 'Pupils must learn that rudeness is not the correct method of expression *but they will not learn this if they are faced with similar rude and punitive expressions from staff* (my emphasis). The good relationships between students and between students and staff in the schools run by the three headteachers described were evidence of a style of leadership which was not only enabling to staff but which placed the interests of students at the heart of the school's activities.

Wisdom

On matters that are controversial or contentious, headteachers require a particular kind of wisdom. It is the wisdom to recognise that teachers are not merely technical experts in particular subjects but people who, although they make mistakes, are sensitive about their personal and professional identities. They are people with values, with beliefs, with a history and culture that has given them a particular perspective on the world. In any attempt to introduce new ideas and change, especially where issues of equity are concerned, it does little if Heads ride roughshod over these individual sensitivities, however much they might disapprove of them. Effective headteachers find ways of reaching out to those least able to understand the changes being introduced.

Racism is a particularly touchy subject for many teachers. The inability, sometimes, to separate motive or intention from the results of one's actions, makes it difficult for some teachers to accept that they need to address racism in their school, so they become angry when students accuse them or their colleagues of racism. In one of the schools I studied for my doctoral thesis, a teacher was so incensed when a student accused her of racism that she declared her willingness to be sacked if the accusations had any truth in them, so sure was she of her own integrity in this matter. But this is where the problem lies – because whilst she was, in her own view and that of her colleagues, a person of integrity, and did not *deliberately* set out to discriminate against black students, several black students interviewed identified her as someone who 'picked on' black students. She may well have been unaware that she was doing so. A girl interviewed for the LEA study said of one teacher:

> I thought Ms Y was racist because I was the only black student and I never done anything, yeah, and yet every time she hears talking she looks at me. So I went to talk to her and she said sorry to me.

This teacher was able to apologise for behaviour she had clearly been unaware of. But what most teachers see are colleagues 'working their socks off' to get students to achieve; they see good, sensitive people struggling against increasing demands from the government and the DfEE; they also see what they perceive to be teachers on the receiving end of black student 'attitude' when their only desire is to treat all their students 'the same'. What they don't see is what the black students themselves perceive, and so they often remain sceptical when students talk about racism.

In their efforts to take all members of staff with them, headteachers need to be aware of these individual and collective beliefs and find strategies based on this knowledge. The first step for them is to understand, with humility and open-mindedness, the perspectives of those who experience racism or other forms of discrimination and to understand that racism also operates through the hidden curriculum. The issue will not be to convince all members of staff that there is racism in the school. There are so many ways for racism to be expressed, and so many different understandings of it, that it would be difficult to arrive at a consensus amongst teachers about the existence of racism in any one institution, let alone in society. What is possibly more common is a view that society might be riddled with racism, but that it does not exist in my school!

Headteachers need to learn from students and their parents by listening to them with an open mind. Then they will have to discuss the issue with staff in a manner which does not leave people defensive and guilty, but which enables them to recognise the myths and contradictions that stare them in the face. When a teacher complained that the Afrikan Studies Department was receiving an unfair allocation of resources, Ms Christian did not get into an argument or accuse anyone of racism but, without making the teacher feel guilty and defensive, examined the allocation book and let the teacher see for herself that this was a myth. When a student accused a teacher of racism, she did not ask the teacher simply to accept that she had been racist but instead asked her to examine the relevant incident and try to understand why the student experienced it in the way she did. What was it, from the student's point of view, that made the incident have this effect on her?

Headteachers are generally supportive of their staff, and as I have indicated earlier, are more likely to support their staff, whether they are right or wrong, than listen to what students have to say. In the studies I have carried out, I found that headteachers are more likely to tackle difficult issues *with wisdom* if the motivation is justice and not only a desire to avoid antagonising staff or to keep the peace. It is generally easier and safer to leave students feeling enraged – when all is said and done, they can always be excluded – than to leave a teacher feeling enraged and risk the wrath of the Unions or other members of staff. Wise handling of problems means taking an approach which does not hedge around or fudge the issue but which also leaves individuals feeling that they have integrity.

Courage

A headteacher talked about how he thought monitoring examination results by ethnicity and gender was a good thing but how he felt unable to introduce it because some members of staff, including the Deputy Head, were opposed to the idea. Another headteacher mentioned his feeling of uncertainty about the justice of expelling a student, but said he had done it because he feared the repercussions from certain members of staff if he did not expel this student. A third headteacher was afraid to set up a meeting of black parents, despite the very specific issues raised by them, lest this antagonise white parents. There are no doubt many more such examples around. These are not easy decisions to make, and it could be argued that headteachers in multi-ethnic schools require greater courage than other headteachers in order to pursue policies and practices that might not have the support of many teachers and parents (Blair, 2001).

Headteachers, however, do have to make decisions that are not necessarily going to be popular but will ultimately benefit the students or the school as a whole. To begin with, the headteacher has to be fully and properly informed about the issues about which a decision has to be made. Without proper understanding of what is involved, and what effects will result from a particular decision, it is difficult to convince staff of the validity of that decision. For example, ethnic and gender monitoring should not be introduced in order to please a lobby of black parents or feminists. There are good academic and moral reasons for introducing monitoring and it is that fact of which headteachers need to be informed and convinced.

Where headteachers believe in what they are doing, there is no need to ride roughshod over people's wishes, neither need they capitulate to the hard-liners. This is what I consider 'strong' about strong leadership. It requires understanding what it is that people are afraid of and then addressing that fear and demonstrating the correctness of one's actions. This does not mean that every single individual will be won over but, as one headteacher in the DfEE study observed, if you persuade people that your idea is worth a try and could be abandoned if it failed, then people will generally go along. If the idea was a good one in the first place, then it is likely that it will succeed in its aims. But a great deal depends on the actual suggestion or decision being made. Where issues impinge on an individual's values and beliefs, it might not be possible to win them over by persuasion or even actual demonstration of the validity of the action. Sometimes, and especially where controversial issues are concerned, it requires the headteacher to be supported by enough people who think the same way, in order to have something implemented, and then to go ahead and implement it and to have the courage to persevere. This can mean that success is not evident until many of the opposers have left the school and new staff are employed on the basis of, amongst other things, values and beliefs which are in keeping with the school's approach.

Courage is a quality which was found to be particularly important in matters of race and ethnicity. Many headteachers will go along, albeit reluctantly, with following edicts about ethnicity laid down by the government or the DfEE. But they are not willing to consider anything more for fear of antagonising white parents and their staff. Even in situations where the black students may not be performing well in school or are over-represented in exclusion, ethnicity is considered to be a touchy subject which is best left alone. So it takes courage for a headteacher to introduce anything that might be considered radical. It takes courage to suggest that high exclusion rates of black students may be symptomatic of institutional racism and that the problem might need to be looked at in that light.

But it is being done in some schools. Headteachers who are oriented away from punishment and who place students, rather than league tables, at the centre of the school's priorities, do find ways of preventing disciplinary exclusions by working with teachers, students and parents. Some schools involve teachers and students together in drawing up a code of behaviour for the school. This behaviour code then applies to all members of the school community, whether teaching staff, ancillary staff, students or parents. Students thus feel a sense of ownership of the rules and a sense of belonging to the school. Some secondary schools take their new students away on an induction weekend where relationships with staff are established and basic rules of respect, behaviour and conflict resolution are worked out together. Some such away-days involve focus on 'discipline' and staff and students in different Year groups work together to draw up a Code of Behaviour for the school. The involvement of parents is also important. When the staff at Catholic School were drawing up an antiracist policy for the school, Ms Christian sought advice from the black parents and the local Racial Equality Council, as well as taking account of what she had learnt from students. These views were included in the draft policy which was then circulated to all parents for comments. A similar procedure was adopted for the anti-sexist policy.

Leadership in multiethnic contexts

The qualities outlined above are important for all headteachers, regardless of context. But they are particularly required of those who have to make decisions on issues of fairness and equality. Leadership in this context requires headteachers to place themselves in the position of those who are least served, or feel they are least served, by the school. The headteachers have to place diversity at the centre of their thinking and be aware of the differential power relations and the differential access to resources that are part and parcel of diversity. In other words, headteachers have to think in multi-dimensional ways. It is no longer appropriate to think in terms of 'how we have always done things'. The idea that all students should be treated the same, that business should go on as usual and difference be dismissed as an irritant, is inappropriate. The headteachers who are able to see things from the perspective of the persons or groups least able to identify with what is happening in the school, are those who are most likely to develop a conviction of the need for change towards social justice.

In an attempt to examine more closely the ways in which black students might be disadvantaged in relation to discipline, I return to the example of Mr Friend, discussed above. We look now at some of the processes in his school, Central City Comprehensive but, more importantly, at his own perspectives and how they affected black students. It is important to point out that neither Mr Friend nor his school is unusual. Indeed, in some ways, Mr Friend exemplifies a headteacher who is more enlightened than many.

Central City Comprehensive (PhD study, written up in 1998 from fieldwork carried out in 1994-1996)

Figures taken from school records show that between 1993 and 1995 thirty-four students of all ethnicities were permanently excluded at Central City Comprehensive. The exclusion reports for these students were scrutinised. Analysis of these reports shows that the students who were expelled fell into four main categories.

1. Students deemed to experience emotional and behavioural difficulties, whose 'needs' were said to have fallen victim to resource cuts, which meant that the school could no longer cater for their specific requirements. These students either had statements of special needs, were having statements prepared, or it was explicitly stated in the student's report that they would be better catered for in a specialised school.

2. Students who were school refusers and for whom the school claimed to have exhausted its efforts to motivate and help them. They seldom came to school and were said to be a 'corrosive' influence on others when they did.

3. Students who were said to behave badly and to have accumulated several referrals and/or exclusions but who were neither school refusers nor said to experience emotional or learning problems

4. Students who were not school refusers, had no learning or behavioural difficulties and no accumulation of exclusions or referrals but who had committed a single offence considered sufficiently serious to merit expulsion.

Table 1 shows the distribution by ethnic group of students in each of the four categories. It shows that most of the students who were expelled from the school during this period were said to have special needs for which the school claimed to be unable to cater.

The two School Refusers listed were both white. Not only had they truanted to a high level but they were deemed to have rejected school altogether. One was said to have a job in his uncle's motor mechanics shop and did not see the relevance of school. The other, whose family was visited by the headteacher, was described as 'a bit of a jack the lad' whose father encouraged his rebellion because 'he did not himself see the relevance of school'.

Table I

Special Educational Circumstances (SEC); NSC (No Special Circumstances)
SR (School Refusers); One-Off

	SEC	NSC	SR	ONE-OFF	TOTAL
African	2	0	0	0	2
Caribbean	7	6	0	2	15
Arab	2	1	0	0	3
Bangladeshi	4	2	0	0	6
Other	1	0	0	0	1
White/European	5	0	2	0	7
Total	21	9	2	2	34

The two one-off offenders were both black (Caribbean) males. Although each had on occasion been sent to the Withdrawal Room during their time at the school, they had not, according to their records,
truanted or disrupted the learning of others, nor had they ever been
excluded. Both were said by teachers to be academically able and
one was in the sixth form. Both students were also said to have
deeply regretted what they had done and to have shown remorse. In
one case, the student (Alan) had been threatened many times by a
group of ex-students (themselves recruited and encouraged by a
rival of Alan's in the school). In an interview, Alan said that he had
reported the threats to a member of staff but had received no support.
He finally decided to bring a meat cleaver into school to defend himself from the group, who waited for him at the school gate and had
threatened to beat him up after school. In the fight that ensued
between Alan and his group of attackers, the meat cleaver fell to the
ground without his having used it, and he was beaten badly enough
to suffer concussion and be taken to hospital. He was expelled on the
basis that he had brought a weapon into school against strict school
rules.

The second case concerned a fight between two students. The
student who was expelled (David) 'viciously' attacked another
student during a quarrel. The other student fell and hit his head and

had to be hospitalised. David had, until then, had a relatively clean discipline record. He apologised, was willing to make amends and visited the victim in hospital. According to the records, this was not the only recorded 'vicious' attack by one student on another. The penalties were, however, differentially applied, as I shall discuss further.

The most interesting feature about Table 1 is that most of the students in the NSC category, namely those who were permanently excluded for 'bad' behaviour without the extenuating circumstances of 'special needs', are African Caribbean. It is worth noting that it is within the NSC category that there is least room for objective judgement to be made regarding student behaviour and therefore most room for arbitrary and inconsistent application of the rules. It is in this category that teachers are most likely to make 'interpretive' rather than 'routine' judgements of student behaviour (Gillborn, 1990). In Gillborn's study, his observations of how and why students were disciplined at City College revealed clear differences in the way teachers assessed the behaviour of African Caribbean students compared with that of students from other groups. White students were more likely to be disciplined for routine (i.e. generally understood) rule breaking (more consistent with Special Educational Circumstances?), whereas judgements about whether African Caribbean students had broken rules tended to be based on the teacher's subjective interpretation of the student's actions.

An examination of the reasons why students had been excluded for a *fixed* term during this period of 1993 to 1995 revealed some of the discrepancies in the manner in which rules were applied. In his explanation of why Alan had been excluded, Mr Friend insisted that all students who brought weapons or drugs to school were *without exception* expelled. He maintained that he was uncompromising about this. However, the list below of reasons for the exclusion of students during this period for drug or weapon-related offences indicates otherwise. Only those offences which included weapons or drugs are listed here.

Bangladeshi	possession of a knife	3 days
White	possession of a knife	3 days
Pakistani	possession of offensive weapon	9 days
African	possession of catapult	3 days
Arab	possession of an axe	9 days
Arab	possession of a gun	4 days
Caribbean	possession of a replica gun	3 days
White	possession of a Stanley knife	2 days

As not one of these students was permanently excluded for these offences, it is difficult to understand why, given his good record of achievement and behaviour and the fact that he had appealed to a teacher for help on account of the threats he had been receiving, Alan was permanently excluded.

There were also discrepancies in relation to illegal substances similar to those relating to weapons. An African Caribbean student was permanently excluded for **suspicion** of selling illegal substances, yet other offences listed were:

Bangladeshi – possession of **illegal** substance	5 days
Caribbean – possession of **unknown** substance	9 days
White – **continued evidence of substance abuse**	6 days

It is notable that both African Caribbean students were given harsher penalties than their white or Bangladeshi counterparts and yet there is no evidence that they did indeed either sell or possess illegal substances. The report on one student records only **suspicion** and for the second student also it seems that there was only suspicion, as the nature of the substance in question was unknown. This makes telling comparison with the case of the other students for whom evidence of illegal substances was indisputable.

In a context in which there is little flexibility for teachers to develop the human and humane elements of their jobs (Grace, 1995), and where pastoral skills are increasingly sacrificed to technical com-

petences, vulnerable groups, namely those whose learning requirements demand more time and imagination from the teacher, or who
have been historically subject to negative stereotyping, are more
likely to be viewed as children 'who should not be in our school'
(Haberman, 1995). Black students are particularly vulnerable to this
kind of assessment, as discussed in Chapter three.

What understanding did Mr Friend have of black students? In an
interview with him, he explained that he thought black (Caribbean)
young people and white working class young people had similar
cultures.

> **Mr Friend**: They spend a large amount of time, if not much of their
> childhood, in groups. They seem to spend much less time in their
> homes in the evenings, and this is the same as the white working class.
> These groups establish a street culture which totally dominates them
> and they have to act up to that style.
>
> ...(The African-Caribbean youth culture) is similar to the white work-
> ing class but is overlaid by a particular Afro-Caribbean flavour which I
> can't quite analyse. They are just not allowed to admit to any kind of
> worry. It masculinizes them and thus is continued in school. Bangla-
> deshis are becoming a problem. They are beginning to cause problems
> across London. But there are some observable differences. The Afro-
> Caribbeans are similar to the white working class, but the package is
> different. Colour is part of it because there is evidence of prejudice.
> They are also brought up from an early age to believe that the world
> is against them and that they have to be against the world.
>
> **MB**: So you think the fault lies in the families?
>
> **Mr. Friend**: I don't think it's anything to do with single parenting. I'm
> inclined to hold exactly the opposite view and say that those who
> don't have the male role model at home might do slightly better than
> those with a male example.

Mr Friend also felt that working class children were not exposed to
the subtleties of the English language and were therefore unable to
negotiate their way in the world in a manner which gained them
sympathy and understanding. I asked Mr Friend why, if white working class cultures and black working class cultures were essentially

the same, black students nonetheless experienced higher exclusions than white students. He replied that:

> Afro-Caribbeans have a two-way attitude to authority. On the one hand, it is quite subservient, and on the other it is belligerent. In a funny way, I think that boys are more subservient yet more likely to knock against authority as opposed to using negotiation. These boys actually assign more power to certain people than those people actually have, and then they knock against it. They knock against it because they elevate this authority to be more powerful than it is.

This discussion seems to me to signal a genuine attempt by Mr. Friend to understand black students in all their complexity, rather than espousing the one-dimensional presentations of most assumptions and stereotypes about black people or, more precisely, black men. However, whatever validity there may be in some of what he says, his thesis is heavily premised on a white middle class norm which casts the working classes of all ethnicities in Britain in the role of deviants (see Sharp and Green, 1975; Keddie, 1984).

Black males, when viewed from such a perspective, appear to be in multiple jeopardy. As black people, they face prejudice and so, in protecting themselves, they learn to become over-sensitive about their colour. As male, they do not receive the same level and quality of nurturing as girls and therefore depend on negative macho street cultures for their sense of identity. As working class, they do not learn the nuances and subtleties of the English language which would help them negotiate their way in the world. As young people, the very adults they ought to look to for examples, namely black men, have themselves been socialised in the same way, and so seldom offer a different, more positive role model. All this positions black young males tenuously and paradoxically in relation to the white middle class world of schools. For these reasons, and particularly because of the absence of the social graces to help them negotiate the world, black boys in school are more likely to 'knock against' authority. The implication seems to be that this accounts for the differential levels of punishment which they receive because it is not only the deed, but the manner in which it is discussed and negotiated, that gets black males into disproportionately greater trouble.

Importantly, Mr Friend does not act on his observations and engage with them in order to prevent students being excluded. He could, under the circumstances, have talked to the black students he considered most vulnerable to exclusion and made them understand the consequences for their futures of being excluded or of failing to gain academic qualifications. This would best be done in a manner which was not disciplinarian but which shows the students that the headteacher cares about them. In some schools a personal show of interest has been shown to work (Blair and Bourne, 1998). Black students have been known to respond well to approaches which do not incessantly remind then of how bad they are and how upset and disappointed everyone is with them, or how they are making life difficult for everybody when everybody is only interested in helping them. Black students feel angered and betrayed when their school experience consists of constant reprimand and little if any praise, when they feel constantly picked on, and when they believe that the teachers do not care about them and are intent only on controlling them.

Mr Friend's theory does not explain why black girls, despite the more supportive nurturing which they supposedly receive and the fact that they are less likely to be influenced by macho street cultures, are nevertheless more likely than white girls to be suspended and expelled from school (see Social Exclusion Unit, 1998). The focus on the cultural aspects of the behaviour of working class young males, and of black males, obscures the impact of the wider society, and indeed of schools, on the educational experiences of young people (Noguera, 1996). It also, as already stated, ignores the ideological orientation and power of headteachers to expel students from or retain them in school.

The hearing at Central City Comprehensive does not present an example of a headteacher who will do all in his power to ensure that students are given every opportunity to correct their behaviour so that exclusion is indeed the final act of despair on his part. The overwhelming message is that black students are sometimes excluded because they do not have the cultural capital to negotiate in acceptable ways with teachers and others in authority. A major problem for black students, Mr Friend argues, is their lack of social graces and communication skills. One might argue that if the primary interests of the student and the purpose of education are considered, these skills should be taught in school. That external constraints place headteachers in a dilemma with regard to exclusion is not denied. Mr Friend himself stated in an interview that, ultimately, he has to do what his teachers want him to do, especially in a context where teachers face considerable stress and might go on strike if their views about certain students are not heeded. However, this argument would in general be much stronger if the debates around the exclusion of black children from school were a recent phenomenon specific to the post-1988 Education Reform Act. Black children in British schools were over-represented in suspensions and expulsions long before the introduction of the National Curriculum, indicating that over and above the difficulties created for schools and teachers by official edicts, there is a need to examine the racialised nature of education and incorporate this into all attempts to understand what is going on.

Conclusion

What I have emphasised in this chapter is that headteachers, as the people with responsibility for keeping or permanently excluding students, can choose to exercise agency on behalf of students. Although the task often presents headteachers with difficult choices, especially where issues of race and ethnicity are concerned, the vital starting point for student success and for prevention of major infringements of school rules is the commitment the headteacher and staff show towards them. This may be stating the obvious, but it can no longer be taken for granted in an age of league tables and within the context of an education market place. Commitment involves believing in the potential of all students and dealing with them with compassion and understanding.

Commitment to students requires re-orienting attitudes and approaches to student misdemeanours so that the school is seen as the place where students will be helped to understand a different way of doing things, rather than as a place which sorts out the deserving from the undeserving. It demands a particular kind of strength on the part of headteachers to question and to challenge the received wisdom of the day in relation to the role of teachers and students in schools, and it requires wisdom to deal fairly with the diverse and conflicting demands of the job. It demands courage to make just decisions and to make them because they *are* just and not because it is a special favour to, or special treatment of, a particular group. Understanding the distinction between justice and special treatment is what is important. What should be done if white girls are the biggest underachieving group in the school? What should be done if black boys are excluded disproportionately to their numbers? What should be done if teachers have low expectations of, say, the Pakistani or the Bangladeshi students? What should be done if the Traveller students face racial harassment or discrimination? These are group factors and require group solutions, and headteachers need the leadership qualities which will enable them to take the affirmative action that can reverse these detrimental trends.

5

Through students' eyes

Interviews I have conducted with black students in a variety of secondary schools across England have confirmed that they feel a great deal of confusion and rage about their schooling, their prospects, and the way they are positioned in society. They are fully aware that education is necessary and important but they are demoralised by a school system which denies them recognition through the curriculum, undermines their sense of self, appears indifferent to their needs, makes learning meaningless and is so intent on controlling them that that they find little to distinguish between schools and detention centres. If schooling was difficult enough in primary school, in the secondary sector it is an obstacle course. Black males in particular see the high levels of unemployment of black men around them and are not inspired by the promise of a better life if they would but conform to a schooling system which marginalises and alienates them, even as it attempts to seduce them with these promises.

All students need more reason to be in school than simply the promise of jobs. What they learn must have some relevance to their personal lives as well as to the world for which they are being prepared. Discipline is a problem because students feel that school is about neither of these things, and the more marginalised they feel, the more irrelevant the whole business of school seems to be. The failure to bring the structure of schooling into the twenty-first century and to define the role of schools in a manner which has meaning for young people, has left them vulnerable to the more seductive attraction offered by the advertising industry, the addictions of consumerism and to many of the dangerous messages coming from films and television (Postman, 1996). A growing sector of the nation's young people is not only alienated from school but finding itself excluded from education because, in the shift from a focus on students to a focus on economic concerns, schools cannot find ways to engage with their needs and concerns. The arena is well prepared for the creation of oppositional cultures and for schools to be, perhaps more than ever before, sites of struggle.

Problems created *for* black students

Many of the difficulties faced by black students are also faced by white (especially working class) students, for the reasons discussed above. Over and above these common experiences, racism was keenly felt by black students. Whilst race was often seen as having a dynamic of its own, social class and gender were seldom recognised or identified as areas of major concern for black students except where, as for example in the experience of black boys, race and gender were seen to be obviously interlinking factors. Fewer girls than boys were interviewed, but these girls identified racism as the most destructive factor in their school lives. A study focusing on how black girls are affected by disciplinary exclusions in school is pressing.

The way forward for schools is to listen to the concerns of students, engage with them and try to resolve them. One of the major problems faced by minority ethnic group students has been not so much blatant racism as liberal complacency and indifference. The majority of teachers are not out-and-out racists, yet this vast body of professionally committed people has allowed the status quo to prevail against the interests of students. In order to resolve the problems of academic failure or underachievement and exclusion, educators need to put aside their defensive stance and the tendency to look outwards for solutions to problems. If schools genuinely want to provide equitable education for their minority ethnic students, they must be prepared to do things differently. In discussions with students about exclusions a number of themes emerged.

Unfair treatment

Several studies in Britain have found that black students are subject to unfair treatment in schools. In his study, Gillborn (1990) observed that teachers used different rules for assessing the behaviours of different groups of students and that these rules were rooted in teachers' racial perceptions of students. Similarly, studies by Wright (1987) and Connolly (1995) illustrated the differential ways in which teachers treated the black students in the early years of schooling, and this was supported by the studies carried out by Mortimore *et.al* (1988) and Tizard *et.al* (1988) both of whose focus was not race but who both concluded that black children were subject to less praise and more reprimands than children from other ethnic groups. Tizard *et.al* state,

> In our interviews with the children, we observed that (black boys) received most disapproval and criticism from teachers, and they were most often said by teachers to have behaviour problems (p.181).

In his study of an infant school, Connolly (1995) argued that black children were constructed as problems by a combination of teacher stereotypes of black people and black men in particular, and the ambivalent attitudes of envy and admiration of their peers. Black boys were thus produced as 'bad' and were likely to be singled out or blamed for incidents in which they had taken no part. He gives a telling example of a boy who was blamed for whistling in class on a day when he was absent from school.

The idea that black children are criticised and reprimanded more because they behave worse than other children therefore needs to be re-examined. The findings of Connolly (1995), Gillborn (1990), Wright *et.al* (2000) and my own studies all suggest that there is indifference, lack of knowledge, and sometimes downright neglect of the educational needs of black students. Anyone wishing to understand the processes that go on in a classroom with black children should read the account by Wright (1992a) of a lesson involving one small black boy, Marcus (p.19-21).

In 1990 when I worked as an Advisory Teacher, I was asked to go to a primary school where a six-year old black boy was said to be causing problems for his teacher. I spent two full days as an 'assistant teacher' in this classroom and what I observed was that, like the children in Wright's study, this boy could not make the slightest move without the teacher noticing and calling him to order. He was the only black child in the classroom and was described by the teacher as so hyper-active that he took up more of her energy than any other child. She felt that he fidgeted during story time, she could hardly get him to sit down in the normal course of the day, and he either wanted to be first in line or else dragged his feet when they had to go to the hall to do PE. When I pointed out to her two children who were at least as – and one of them certainly more – active than the black child, she was surprised at her own perception. One of these boys was the black child's best friend and I once witnessed this friend pulling him back so they *both* dawdled when they should have been going to the school hall. Yet the teacher had perceived the black child as the one who led his friend astray! But what made this boy especially vulnerable was that his behaviour was being interpreted as a characteristic of his race and therefore beyond the teacher's ability to understand or deal with. Had he been seen as just another six year old child, she might have found nothing extraordinary about his behaviour and noted that several other children in the class behaved in much the same way. But even had he been more hyper-active than other children and problematically so, the Multicultural Service was hardly the place to seek help. It was the perception of his behaviour as symptomatic of a racial condition that led to our being called to intervene. His mother (who, as it happened, was white) had observed nothing abnormal about his level of energy.

Black students in secondary school may well have endured similar negative attention at primary school. They gave accounts of being picked on by teachers and thus of being more likely than white students to get into situations of conflict with teachers. Claims by students that they are picked on are common. Many children, from all ethnicities, will tell you that their teacher picks on them, usually adding, 'for no reason'. However, in my interviews with white students, never did I come across one who felt that he or she was picked on because they were white – not even where the teacher in question was black.

Theorists of the self-fulfilling prophecy argue that teachers' expectations invariably affect the way they relate to students. The student in turn reflects these expectations through his or her actions, thereby fulfilling the teacher's original prophecy. When teachers have high expectations of students they respond positively and learning becomes a rewarding and challenging experience for them. However, if a teacher's expectations undermine the student, it causes resentment and alienation and this leads to a negative experience for both teacher and student.

The widespread feeling among students that black students were more likely than white to be picked out for talking or other forms of disobedience in the classroom had a demoralising effect on black students and could become a self-fulfilling prophecy.

> **White student:** I don't think some teachers give out C4s (warnings) fairly because last year, there was a group of boys in our French class and they hadn't even done anything and the teacher gave them C4 after C4 for no apparent reason. They felt like she was just being racist or something and each time they went into a lesson, they went out of their way to annoy her because they felt she had been unfair.

Although the students who took part in these discussions insisted that not all teachers treated black students unfairly, all the black students nevertheless stated that where students of all ethnic groups were involved in messing about or other forms of rule breaking, the black students were most likely to be picked out for reprimand or punishment. This selective form of identification was said by many of those interviewed in the various studies to be not uncommon in schools. And this was the view not only of students but of some teachers, especially black teachers, as well as being confirmed in my own classroom and playground observations.

> **Sean 16 years:** If say, I'm sitting next to a white friend in class and the friend is telling me something, the teacher can hear where the talking is coming from, but instead of looking to see who is actually doing the talking, he'll just call out my name. It's just always me that gets the blame.

I was once observing a science lesson when just such an incident occurred. The teacher heard talking, and turning around, threw a piece of chalk at the sole black student in the class. At this, one girl said to the teacher, 'But Miss, the talking wasn't even coming from where Joe is sitting. You always pick on him'. There was a chorus of support from the other students. The teacher admitted afterwards that she couldn't think why she had thought he was the one who was talking.

Sometimes singling out black students is done deliberately and oppressively.

Tyrone 15 years: My friends and I were just about to go into our classes when Mr C. came and goes, 'You, you and you', calling out the three black boys. And he goes, 'Give me your diaries'. So we said, 'What for? We haven't done anything wrong'. And he says, 'Don't ask me for an explanation. I don't have to give you an explanation. I'm a teacher, and when I ask to see your diaries, you give them to me'.

Glenda, 15 years: Isobel, Lorene and me are really good friends, yeah, and we always used to stick together especially at lunch times. Then this group of white girls started calling us names, racial names and calling us slags, and so we started to call them names. Anyway, it got really bad and Mr Martin, the Deputy Head decided it had to end. So he calls us three black girls and tells us that he never wants to see us together in the playground again, and so every break, Isobel has to go to that corner of the playground, (pointing) I have to go to that one, and Lorene has to go to that one. But the white girls can stay as friends and don't have to split up. And now Isobel hardly ever comes to school and me and Lorene sometimes bunk off because there's just no point coming to school if you can't be with your friends.

Cullingford and Morrison (1997) emphasise the importance of friends in helping young people develop a sense of identity and for 're-inforcing, reflecting, and reciprocating valued aspects of the self' (p.62). The importance of having one's mates to muck about with and generally relieve the boredom of school routine has been discussed by other writers also (see for example Woods, 1990). That these students should have been deprived of the chance to meet with their friends was keenly felt and resented, and, furthermore, removed

78

one of the most important motivations for coming to school at all. But it was the unfair and racialised manner in which the deputy headteacher had solved the problem of the rival groups which rankled most in the minds of the students and was referred to in nearly all the discussions I had with students in this school.

Respect

This was an area of immense concern for students and also their parents, particularly for secondary school students. I mentioned earlier that adolescents may behave in particular ways which are unacceptable and that this is part of the process of growing up and establishing their independence from adults. However, in order to know what is acceptable, they need guidance from the adults with whom they come into contact and especially those who have responsibility over them. If teachers demand respect from students in the form of obedience, not 'cheeking back', not 'cussing' and so on, they need to earn this respect by always setting a good example themselves. We know from what students say that not all teachers earn such respect and that students resent their taking the line of 'do as I say but not as I do'. Many teachers shout at, humiliate and verbally abuse students in behaviour which would gain a student acting similarly a fixed if not a permanent exclusion. Some students have been excluded for less.

I asked ten primary school children in a group interview to say what they most liked or disliked about their school. Being shouted at by teachers was what they hated most. In a survey of 200 Year 10 students, the students listed teacher attitude to them, as expressed through verbal and body language, as the greatest cause of conflict between teachers and students. But although all students were concerned about how they were treated, the notion of respect had a particular meaning for black students.

> **Steven, 14 years**: It was the way he was talking to me. He had no respect for me. I'm not saying I wanted to be treated like an equal, after all I'm only a child, but that's not what I'm saying. He had no *human* respect (original emphasis), like he wasn't talking to another person, you understand what I mean. So I said to him, 'How can you

79

expect me to act like an adult yet you don't even talk to me or respect me like a person who has some intelligence?'

Richard, 15 years: I'm not rude to all teachers, but I'm rude to those who don't show me respect. Who treat me like I'm not a person.

Steven and Richard are quite specific about teachers talking to them as if they were not human. They evidently do not see this as an aberrant form of teacher behaviour – it resonates for them with wider racial discourses which inferiorise black and other minority peoples and devalue their contribution to the world. Teun van Dijk (1993:104) notes that

> Negative opinions about minority groups may be expressed and conveyed by intonation or gestures that may be inconsistent with seemingly 'tolerant' meanings.

Van Dijk calls these forms of behaviour 'offensive speech acts'. To black students such speech acts signalled the 'true intentions and feelings' of teachers, and they were particularly sensitive to their display in public situations. Although all students resent teachers who abuse their power by treating them with disrespect, for black students this abuse of power has a powerful racial dimension which is lived out on a daily basis within and beyond the school gates. But when teachers are told that students (and not only black students) feel disrespected, they generally respond with disbelief and the riposte that 'after all, isn't this just what students would say?' Few schools take the time to find out exactly what students mean when they talk about disrespect. Adolescents are particularly sensitive to being treated like naughty children even if they have done something 'naughty', but especially when they feel that the accusation is unjustified. Barking orders at students or using a tone of voice that implies criticism or put-down, or casting unkind looks, are some of the aspects considered by students to be disrespectful of them. As one student said, 'Teachers don't do that to each other, so why should they do it to us?'

Some schools, however, do take the trouble to find out what students are thinking and feeling. One commissioned a study with their Year 10 students, based on focus group discussions and a questionnaire.

The results surprised the teachers so much that they extended the study to include all Year groups and the results formed the basis of staff INSET days and future policy. Another school has an annual 'retreat' day with all Year 9 students and their tutors, to which they invite outside facilitators and explore different issues together, and these discussions inform the school's academic as well as pastoral policies.

Stereotypes

Stereotypes of black students do not originate in schools but can be traced historically to European theories about 'Others' and how they could make sense of them (Rattansi and Donald, 1992). These theories have led to a variety of stereotypes which affect groups in different ways. For example, while the theory of white superiority provided a particular view of non-white peoples generally, different types of stereotypes were developed in context for different groups at particular moments in history. Black men have been variously represented as violent, aggressive, sexually out of control and en-gaged in illicit activities such as mugging and drug pushing, and these are perceived by black students to inform some of the stereo-types of black boys' behaviour in school.

One sixth form student explicitly equated the assumptions some teachers were said to hold with those he believed to be held by the police. He talked of the 'heavy-handed policing' of black males by teachers. He was of the view that interactions between white teachers and black students were informed by stereotypes of black people in films and the media. Black teachers were different, he said, because '*They understand the situation because they experience it themselves*'. One black 15 year old summed it up like this:

> **Andrew:** Teachers don't treat students with respect anyway, but they have a different approach for black students because they think you're a thief, they think you're violent, they think you're a troublemaker, and from these thoughts... just from the way we're dressed we get stereotyped. A black boy with designer jeans and they want to know where he got them. A friend of mine was in the Withdrawal Room and the teacher was saying, making blatant racist statements saying that he

must have got his expensive clothes from drug money, and that his brother was a thief and his father was a dealer, making racist jokes like that. That's why I argue so much with teachers, because they say such things and I can't find it in myself to treat such teachers with respect.

This statement, spoken with considerable anger, indicates the deep level at which students feel abused by racist stereotypes. At an age when they need positive affirmation of their identity and a sense of their own worth, such 'offensive speech acts' can be nothing less than psychological abuse. Patricia Hill-Collins (1986) contends that stereotypes function to dehumanise and control. Black students felt dehumanised in a number of ways. For example, students offered numerous anecdotes of occasions when teachers assumed that when something went missing, a black student must be to blame.

Lynda, 13 years: We had just gone back to the classroom after PE when Miss James came and asked if she could see me. She took me into the corridor and asked if I had seen this girl's purse which had gone missing from the shower room, so I said, 'but Miss, why have you picked me out to ask?' And she said, 'I'm not picking you out, I intend to ask everybody who used the showers'. So I said, 'No, I haven't seen the purse.' She says, 'Are you sure because things could be a lot worse if you were found to be lying'. And I said, 'I haven't seen it, and I haven't taken it, OK?' and I went back into the class. Then she comes into the class and asks the whole class, she doesn't call anyone else out, she asks the whole class if anyone had seen the purse. They just think we're thieves for no reason.

There were several such examples of black students feeling that they had been unjustifiably singled out and suspected of theft or other forms of dishonesty for no other reason than that they were black.

Cameron, 15 years: Mr Stanley came into the class and came straight over to me and said, 'Where is it? Hand it over'. I didn't even know what he was talking about, but he just took my bag and started searching it. Only later when I was about to go home he came over to me and apologised because someone had lost their personal stereo, and he just assumed it was me (who had taken it).

Mr Stanley may well have been acting on information he received from someone. His own reasons for picking this student out may not have been motivated by racism. But the fact that the student thought so was based on the wider experiences of black people. Historical representations of black people (and other non-white peoples who have experienced colonialism) as dishonest, affected black young people outside of as well as in school. For example, random stop and search policies by police are directed at black people five times more than any other group. This fact is seldom grasped by teachers to inform their relations with or understanding of black students. Mr Stanley should never accuse a student without first making sure of the facts, but his failure to grasp the implications for black students of his accusation is significant. For them this is a particularly sore point which connects to harassment of black people by the police. Victor's experience, which he describes below, indicates how 'you're damned if you do and you're damned if you don't'.

> **Victor, 15 years:** I found a cheque book. I went to hand it in to the police and went home. Next thing they were coming to my house to ask me questions and to accuse me of stealing it.

Stereotypes take various forms. Mirza (1992) describes the racialised, class and gender stereotypes held by the teachers in her study of black girls, and the sexual undertones in the white male teachers' assumptions about them. A negative black femininity is thus produced and reproduced in the school context (Wright *et.al* 2000). Others (see for example Fuller 1984) write about the perceptions of teachers that black girls have 'attitude'. I raised this point in one of my interviews with a group of black girls in the DfEE study (Blair and Bourne, 1998). What Shelley told me epitomises the 'racial frames of reference' (Figueroa, 1991) which inform the understandings of so many teachers:

> **Shelley:** Teachers stereotype us, they stereotype the black students.

> **MB.** What kind of stereotypes do they use?

> **Shelley:** It's just the way they stereotype us. Ms X said to me, 'Don't start any of your Afro-Caribbean attitude with me'. My parents are divorced, I live with my white mother, I've never been to the Caribbean, so what did she mean by that?

It was also felt that certain stereotypes of black students held by teachers are characterised by low academic expectations, and this too leads to a self-fulfilling prophecy.

> Nathan, 17 years: Teachers have preconceived ideas about the abilities of black students. Students pick this up and start reacting negatively. It's usually a build up of negative feeling in the black student and then it goes to a stage where the school wants to get rid of them anyway. So if they do anything, they're out, whereas white students don't have that negative build up.

Black students also confirmed their experience of the common stereotyped view of them as being more able at sports than at intellectual pursuits.

> **Steven, 15 years**: They're always pushing us into sport. When it comes to school work they don't think you can do it and they don't give a damn about you. But when it comes to sport, they love you.

> **Darren, 14 years**: I was excluded once, right, and the school was going to play a football match in the school league. Now everybody knows that I'm really good at football, and of course the teacher wanted me to play in the league, so although I was supposed to be excluded, they decided to end my exclusion so that I could play for the school.

All young people need a sense of achievement to give them direction. In his statement, Steven underlines the insecurity students feel as a result of the selective and racialised way in which they are rated in school and the correlation with how school subjects are valued and hierarchised. If students are black, they are, in Stephen's view, prized not for their intellectual abilities but only for their lower level 'physical prowess' in sport. Darren illustrates how students are aware of the tendency by schools to prioritise behaviour management of black students over their academic achievement, and also of the inconsistent and selective way in which rules are applied when the interests of the school are at stake. That Darren was deemed bad enough to be kept out of school and so miss out on essential subject knowledge but good enough to be allowed back to rescue the football team, raises questions about the legitimacy of some school exclusions. Indeed one parent who was interviewed for the DfEE study considered bizarre the whole notion of sending children home as a punishment rather than suspending them from those school activities to which they had privileged access, such as certain sports.

Racism

In all the interviews, students were careful to differentiate between teachers whom they thought blatantly racist, those who seemed to be ignorant of what constituted racism and those for whom racism was said to operate at an unconscious level. Some students tried to define racism.

> **David:** I don't think it's the kind of racism which says, 'I hate black people'. It's like, they have this feeling about black people which just won't escape from them. It's always there.

> **Brian:** I don't think all white teachers are racist, but it's easy to pick out the ones that are, especially as some of them can be so blatant. There's one teacher, even when I put my hand up first, she goes past me and asks someone else. She does that a lot. I also find that she tries to spend as little time as possible explaining things to me, then she moves on to someone else. It's like, anything I do, however small, it seems to irritate her and she'll make a big thing out of it. I have her for three lessons a week, and I *want* (original emphasis) to go to school, but I feel I can't.

> **MB.** But how can you be sure that what you are experiencing is racism and not a personality clash, say?

> **Brian:** It's the body language. If you've experienced it you know it and can tell the difference between one white person's attitude and another.

> **Jason:** It's the way they speak to you, look at you, degrading you, putting you down. It's difficult to explain. It's more something that you feel but can't describe. And you certainly won't be feeling that way about all white teachers.

David's observation illustrates the way the 'inner eye' operates. Brian's experience exemplifies the processes of exclusion (as opposed to expulsion) which take place in schools. These processes lead to student resentment and alienation, to poor and deteriorating relationships and sometimes ultimately to permanent exclusion. What was certain from my interviews with students was the enormous resentment generated when they felt they had been unfairly treated, especially if this was because of their identities as black people. One student pointed to this resentment as a major source of conflict between teachers and students.

> **Jason:** Any black person that realises what's going on, and I can tell you, no black person I know, no black person who can see that something is obviously happening to them, is going to keep quiet about it. Like in school, we can see these things happening to us, and no black person is going to be quiet when they are pushed down. They'll always say something.

Along with a pervasive feeling that they were placed in a position of disadvantage in relation to their white peers, black students felt that their negative reactions did not match the level and extent of the unfair or unjust treatment meted out to them.

> **Bryn:** Compared with the way teachers 'cut you up', I'd say that black students really hold back a lot, a lot... One teacher told a black girl that she looked like a chimpanzee. She just walked out and I thought, 'Good for you. You don't have to take that from him', and I was cursing him in my mind. He saw the look of anger on my face so he came up and tried to talk about my work, but I just stiffened up and gave him a look which made it clear to him that I wanted him to keep away from me.

Bryn gives a vivid picture of the strong feelings black students have that their identities are being eroded and demeaned. His words encapsulate the vicarious way in which racism was experienced (Essed, 1990). In his statement, Bryn shows how an image of white teachers as racist can take hold in the minds of students. The example he gives underlines the notion that teachers and students may attribute different causes to the same events. In the situation described, the teacher did not direct his offensive remark at Bryn – it was his interaction with another black student that caused his relationship with Bryn to deteriorate. The teacher might attribute Bryn's reaction to an internal cause (a chip on the shoulder or a persecution complex) and not realise that Bryn's reaction was directly triggered by the wider racial implications of the teacher's own racist remark even though he had not targeted Bryn.

Faced with such emotionally corrosive practices in the classroom, it is not unreasonable to conclude that black students will have their ability to concentrate and participate in the classroom severely damaged. Contrast such teacher behaviour with the 'good teachers' of minority students. For these teachers, according to Ladson-Billings (1994): 'Psychological safety is the hallmark of (their) classrooms. The students feel comfortable and supported' (p.73). The link between behaviour and underachievement can be reasonably assumed in situations where students do not feel 'comfortable and supported'.

Gender

In my study for my doctoral thesis, I found that black boys were four times more likely to be expelled from school than black girls (see also Wright *et.al* 2000). This could be partly explained by the fact that teachers operate different stereotypes for girls and boys in co-educational contexts, but partly also by the way that boys and girls generally respond differently to situations. Teachers were perceived by the black students to be drawing on gender differentiated constructions of black people which were prevalent in the wider society. A sixth form girl observed how the internal dynamics of the school combined with external factors to affect black boys more than black girls. She was referring to her own school, which was in an inner city area where black residents experienced high levels of unemployment, poverty and police harassment.

> **Gloria:** The black boys see no point, there's nothing out there for them. Teachers don't motivate them, they leave it up to the students themselves. I know that I'm here to stay, there's nothing I can do about the system. It'll be the same system for my children and grandchildren. So I think about getting the most for myself, even though I don't like it.

Here Gloria underlines a significant point made by Mirza (1992). Girls are more likely to view their schooling as an important foundation for not only the world of work but for their future responsibilities as mothers. Black girls, according to Mirza, expect to be the primary carers of their future children and do not necessarily expect that they will have a man living with them. They are also very conscious of the fact that black men experience high levels of unemployment, and do not therefore assume that the fathers of their children will be in a position to support them. They have to think beyond the immediate relationships they have with teachers and make use of strategies which will help them survive the barriers and obstacles thrown up by racism. Boys, faced with the challenge to their masculine pride in their interactions with teachers and others in authority in the school (Mac an Ghaill, 1994), and faced with evidence that they are not likely to share in the rewards which an education gives to their white peers, are less likely to adopt passive forms of resistance in order to preserve their 'racial' identities.

This is not to say that girls are necessarily passive nor that all boys respond in the same way to certain situations. Gillborn (1990) for example, reported on black males who tried to keep a low profile (see also Fordham, 1996) and chose to avoid the teachers with whom they were likely to have conflict, rather than have to face the need to defend their honour and dignity by reacting to situations which they found intimidating. Mac an Ghaill (1988), amongst others, writes about the different forms of resistance that girls use which allow them the room to achieve academically. However, it seems from the evidence presented by these studies that black males are targeted more than black girls for discipline in co-educational contexts, whilst black girls are targeted more than white girls. Black girls' experience of discipline is clearly an area for further research and analysis.

In a discussion with a group of 15 year old boys about how boys got into trouble more than girls did, one of them commented that, 'Girls are more sensible and think about the consequences. They are more calm. Boys act hard'.

This group of boys presented a nonchalant stance, partly, one presumes, because of the need to maintain a 'hard' image by presenting the other side of hardness – being 'cool' (see Majors and Billson, 1992). But when I talked to some of them individually where they were not under pressure to protect their masculine image, they came across as vulnerable and nothing like as tough as they wanted to appear.

> **Bryn:** The white boys expect us to be tough all the time. And sometimes you might just be feeling really scared inside, but you can't show it.

Mr Friend, the headteacher at Central City Comprehensive, was particularly aware of this need to appear tough, though he seemed unaware of what he, the headteacher could do to help and support black boys.

> **Mr Friend:** Black boys are cast into roles of being tough. They are not allowed to be sensitive and gentle. They are not allowed to admit to any kind of nervousness or tentativeness or to admit that they are worried about anything.

What could Mr Friend have done? It is often assumed that the only answer is to find black mentors for the students. This seems to me to be opting out rather than seeking real solutions. Black mentors can be only part of the solution. Some schools take affirmative action in relation to building relationships with the students by, for example, finding mentors from *amongst the teachers*, or whole departments targeting these students and helping to build their self-confidence, monitor their work, be available to help them and constantly making it clear that they have high expectations of them. For any students who have fallen behind in a subject, teachers arrange extra revision and persuade the students that they are willing to help them catch up and achieve. Some schools work with the 'leaders', encouraging them to attend revision and 'bring their mates along', and alongside all this goes plenty of praise and encouragement. This is important for a group of students who normally experience school as a place in which they have no sense of belonging. Most important, however, is caring. If students do not feel that all this is being done because the teachers care about them, they will see it as just another control mechanism. The good practice must therefore be rooted in staff teamwork, with an agreed series of strategies and consistency of application, accompanied by high positive expectations. The aim must be to build an environment in which students feel psycho-logically safe and comfortable.

Problems created by black students

There was never, in my discussions, any attempt by black students or their parents to deny that the students broke rules or committed offences that deserved sanction. What they did refute was the notion that black students as a racial or ethnic group behaved differently from how white students would behave in similar circumstances. This perception, they felt, arose from the fact that when a black student did something wrong, it was more likely to be interpreted as symptomatic of 'blackness' and so of all black students than as a problem of the individual. Whereas when white students did some-thing wrong, it was seen as a problem of that individual, not as symptomatic of 'whiteness'. The overwhelming response from students was that black students as a group did not create any more problems for schools than did their white counterparts, but that their behaviours were interpreted as more problematic not because they *were* so but because teachers either did not understand them or were less tolerant of anything the black students did. In other words they were less likely to conform to teachers' notions of the ideal student and were thus constructed as a problem by teachers (see also Wright *et.al* 2000). Being more likely to get into trouble or having higher levels of exclusion should thus not be interpreted as evidence that it is black students who behave worst.

Explanations for their disproportionate exclusion varied from one context to another, and according to the ethnic group of teacher, the teacher's awareness of racial politics or the general ethos of the school. This variation indicates that racial or ethnic explanations for poor behaviour lie mainly with the perceptions of the school or the teachers in it, rather than being a problem created by students' be-haviour. This is not to deny that some teachers do face more problems with their black students. But as the accounts in this chapter have shown, any understanding would require close and detailed scrutiny not only of what the students do but also of the context in which they are experiencing their education.

Context

In a shire (county) school with 3% black students, 1% South Asian students and the rest white, black students constitute 25% of all exclusions. In another inner city metropolitan school, with 3% black students, 51% South Asian students and 45% white students, black students are amongst the highest achievers and teachers could think of only one black student who had had a fixed exclusion in the previous three years. In a church school with 30% black students, the focus was on prevention and there had been no exclusions in three years. Black students in this school were said to be achieving as well and in some subjects better than their white peers. In another church school, the 30% black students were disproportionately over-represented in exclusions. Here black students were described as posing a serious disciplinary problem for teachers, and also as academically underachieving.

For schools to understand what is going on in relation to ethnicity and discipline, each has to examine its own context but also understand the wider context in which black students are over-represented in disciplinary exclusions. It is important to reflect upon whether interpretations of behaviour are based on a racial frame of reference or whether each student is perceived as an individual, and whether the personal circumstances, age and learning needs of each is taken into account. But most importantly, each school needs to reflect on its own ethos and the extent to which it subscribes to the current culture of punishment in British schools. It is also important in situations of recurring conflict to examine the history of each teacher's relations with black students.

Students identified a number of factors which characterised teachers who picked on them or were quick to apply disciplinary warnings or punishments. These were the teachers who could not control their

WHY PICK ON ME? SCHOOL EXCLUSION AND BLACK YOUTH

classes, who felt intimidated by students, especially those who challenged their knowledge, who felt threatened by the stereotype of black students as troublemakers and, significantly, the teachers who gave boring lessons.

> **Turkish Girl**: If a lesson is boring, you can't pay attention so you want to chuck things around and have a bit of fun.

> **Black Boy**: In a boring lesson, they are more likely to do what they want and not pay attention. They would most probably want to take advantage of the teacher.

> **White Boy**: He's boring. Even though he teaches a subject which could be so interesting, he makes it so boring.

For their part, the teachers attributed certain problems specifically to black students or claimed that they were more prevalent among them. The teachers' statements below are representative. One black woman teacher said:

> It really upsets me to see the way they behave. It's almost as if they have to prove something, you know, I am the greatest, I can beat you all up, I am the coolest kid on the block.

A white woman teacher declared:

> I think they are quicker to confrontation. Their reactions to situations are often more extreme, either through the kind of language they use or their body language. I also think that African-Caribbean kids in the school are more street, more keen to have an image. I'm not saying they necessarily want to have a bad image, but image is very important, kudos, street cred is important.

A white PE teacher described the behaviour of some of the black students as 'bizarre':

> I've got a GCSE group and there are three Afro-Caribbeans in there. All extremely able. Physically able, there's no doubt about that, but also academically able. But their behaviour is most bizarre. One of them needs to seek attention all the time, and I've said to him that if he behaved like that outside he'd be arrested. There's another kid who I think wants to succeed, but because he's mates with the other two,

he's got to be seen to be, you know, bouncing about, jack the lad, not conforming, pushing the limits.

A black male Head of Department said this:

...a lot of black boys are very macho and the way they act is very challenging. They are often defiant to authority because they have a lot of negative feelings towards school. But I also think a large number of teachers feel challenged by, or physically threatened by black pupils and they don't challenge their behaviour.

I would like to look more closely at these statements by teachers, both white and black, in order to understand the nature of the difficulties they say that black students cause. Three main surmises emerge:

- that black students' responses to situations are more extreme and that they are quicker to be confrontational

- that black students are obsessed with image and it is not street cred to be academic

- that they are macho and some teachers find this threatening.

Variations of these statements were made by other teachers, and were largely admitted by students themselves. So we need to take them seriously in order to understand how best to respond to black students or how to change a situation which is clearly detrimental to them. These statements and others in this vein were made mainly about boys, though the statement about students' quick reactions referred equally to the girls.

The first assumption can be interpreted in three ways. Black students are either *biologically* (i.e. it is a function of their race) extreme and confrontational – in which case all black students behave this way and nothing can be done about it – or black students *face situations* which arouse quicker and more extreme responses, or *respond* this way for the sake of their image.

Diversity within black communities and among black students rules out the first explanation. Not all black students respond confrontationally to every situation, as many teachers attested. Black students themselves, and teachers, pointed to black students who were 'passive' in their responses (cf. Gillborn 1990). They also identified students who had particular emotional needs and who responded no differently from white students with similar needs. Indeed for a biological explanation to be valid, evidence would have to exist of unfailingly extreme responses from black students the world over!

On the second premise, research has established that black students are often placed in situations in which they are made to feel debased. In such cases, it is the institution and the people with power that are in effect 'the problem', not the students. As the teacher above re-marked, black students have a good many negative feelings towards schools. Some writers would argue that what the students are doing is resisting the power and control being unfairly exercised over them (Sewell, 1997; Wright *et.al.*, 2000). The focus for change would have to be to *remove the conditions* which lead to such responses from black students.

It seems unlikely that black students in all their diversity and dispersed locations would respond in specific ways for the sake of their image. And this surmise assumes that young people of other ethnic groups care nothing about image. The same flaw exists in the surmises about black students needing street cred and being macho. In all considerations of such statements, it is important to bear in mind that these are always generalisations, because the descriptor 'black' is applied to people from many different countries, cultures, languages, religions and so on. And there is as much diversity bet-ween students of different Caribbean heritages as there is between students with the same Caribbean heritages.

Although teachers in my various studies did identify macho charac-teristics as being more prevalent among black (male) students than among whites or South Asians, it is often the case that where one or a few black students are highly visible and voluble their behaviour is seen as characteristic of all black students. In one school where the student population was predominantly Pakistani, a teacher described the behaviour of the boys in the very same terms used to describe black boys elsewhere. Furthermore, when teachers in the various schools were asked if there were any black students who did not behave in these ways, it invariably turned out that *most* black students *did not* and that the teachers had been referring to only a particular group of friends, or to a couple of individuals who were usually identified as having problems.

This does not mean that we should not take teachers' concerns seriously. A number of them thought, for example, that the music and dance cultures which influence black students were responsible for a peer group culture in which these characteristics are more widely displayed than in other groups. It is certain however from what the students say, that whatever specifically black peer group cultures emerge, these are, possibly in large part, a response to racialised perceptions and expectations of black students (boys) by their peers or by teachers, (see Connolly 1995), or to a sense of displacement in the society at large. Black students are expected to be cool, to be 'tough', to defy authority, and they will often find themselves under pressure to prove that they are all these things. Music lyrics which are homophobic and sexist simply provide them with an outlet for expressing forms of masculinity already produced through subtle and nuanced ways in the hidden curriculum and by a racialised and gendered schooling system (Mac an Ghaill, 1994; Connolly, 1995).

While carrying out a study for an LEA, I was waiting outside the office of the Head of Year when a group of Year 8 students came to line up in the corridor where I stood. I heard a white student say to a black student, 'I dare you to let off the fire extinguisher'. The black student replied, 'Why don't you do it yourself, why should I get into trouble?' Black students are generally not expected to give responses of this kind. The image, therefore, may not be what they actively seek but what some of them feel they have to uphold because this is what the world expects of them (see Wright *et.al.*, 2000) for an excellent discussion about the interaction of race, class and gender in the experience of black students).

If black students do create more problems in some contexts, then the solution would seem to be for teachers and schools as institutions to try to understand the pressures on young people, the racial and ethnic dimensions of such pressure, and to find ways of overcoming these pressures rather than punishing the students. The question would have to be: 'what is it about our particular context that causes black students to be confrontational and feel they have to prove themselves?' What also needs to be asked is this: if the adolescent peer group does exert more pressure on black boys than white, why is there over-representation of black students among those excluded even in infant and primary schools (see Hayden, 1997) and even in areas with small numbers of black students and where the black peer group does not appear to be an issue for teachers or students? Most importantly, what can be done about the disproportionate application of this sanction?

Certainly there are students who push teachers to the limits of their patience and endurance. Some writers (see for example Rise-borough, 1984) warn against positioning students as the 'victims' of teacher behaviour. They underline the importance of viewing students as agents in their own lives, capable of subverting teacher intentions. Through their behaviour, such children can 'critically affect the teacher's health and survival and the degree of stress that the teacher experiences' (Riseborough, 1984, pg. 17). Interactions in the classroom are a two-way process. The context of teaching is un-doubtedly important for deciding the nature and outcomes of these relationships. A racialised environment, where racism is a factor in the school as well as outside, is bound to compound the negative effects of this dialectic relationship between teachers and students. But ultimately, teachers have overall power to decide the fate of students through the sanction available to them of exclusion.

Conclusion

In all these discussions, black students did not deny that they some-times broke rules, or indeed that some black students – like students from all groups – caused severe problems for the learning of others. What was found to be unacceptable were the multiple assumptions about black people which informed teacher-student interactions and which could so easily lead to unjust decisions.

The practice of singling out black students, whether consciously or unconsciously, for differential treatment, has important implications for exclusion. If black students are singled out for extra surveillance and control, or given harsher treatment than others, they are more likely to receive a disproportionate number of disciplinary referral forms. And my various studies have all shown that they do. These referral forms are taken into account in decisions about whether a student should be temporarily excluded, permanently excluded, or given another chance, and the more referral forms a student has, the greater the likelihood of permanent exclusion. If black students in any school are seen as creating the most difficulties for teachers, it is essential to understand why this should be the case. But before any kind of analysis can take place, all racial explanations would have to be discarded. These are invalid and lead down the alley of the stereotype. Real understanding will only come with real commitment to make a difference and therefore with real listening followed by acting honestly on what is learnt. There are important questions that all those working in a school have to ask and then act upon in order to change the experiences of both the teachers and the students.

6
Teachers' roles and responsibilities

S o far, I have argued against excluding students from school.
I've shown how different forms of exclusion in the hidden
curriculum and in disciplinary measures, reflect unjust practices and result in the reproduction of social inequality in schools. To
position myself thus, however, implies that there are pedagogic practices and other ways of relating to students which do not have these
effects or which can at least reduce them. In Chapter Four, I discussed how important the ideological orientation of the headteacher
is in deciding the fate of students. I argued that students' lives could
be affected in positive or negative ways, depending on whether or
not the welfare and interests of the students were placed at the centre
of disciplinary decisions. In this chapter I examine the ideological
orientation of teachers and discuss ways teachers might affect the
emotional and academic welfare of their students, particularly black
students.

It is worth re-stating some of the difficulties faced by teachers today.
We noted earlier the pressures and restrictions faced by teachers as
a result of the educational changes of the last decade or so. The time
teachers can spend on individual students has been severely eroded.
Resources which were traditionally drawn upon to support both
teachers and students have been curtailed or withdrawn altogether.
Teachers are under pressure to prove their technical competence at
the expense of the moral development and values education of their
students. The structures of the schooling system do not afford the
time and space for teachers and students to develop in the crucial
area of relationships. We have also noted how teachers themselves

are neglected in terms of diversity education at college, and the absence of antiracist, anti-sexist and other forms of education for social justice. The little in-service education on these issues is generally seriously inadequate and seldom has long-term effects. Instead of being trained to prevent misbehaviour, teachers, according to Haberman (1995) are

> ...trained to escalate, i.e. warn, withdraw a privilege, administer a negative consequence, remove, suspend, and finally evict. Not only are such procedures ineffective, but the number of at-risk, disruptive, and failing students is skyrocketing as more and more teachers use more and more punishments. In truth, the possible rewards adolescents receive from peers for noncompliance are more powerful than any of the school's punishments. (p. 7).

A number of educationists, (Fine, 1991; Ladson-Billings 1994; Cullingford *et.al* 1997) contend that the way teachers see their jobs and their attitudes towards their students affect how they carry out their professional work. Haberman (1995) and Ladson-Billings (1994) each outlined the features they found to contribute to teachers' effectiveness with students from minority ethnic groups. Both found the attitudes the teachers held towards their students to be significant, along with their ability to respect their students' identities and to provide teaching which was culturally relevant and also engaging. Teachers in Britain, as I have argued, are not given adequate preparation in these matters. This is reflected not only in the high levels of exclusion from school but especially in the over-representation of black students in exclusions. Some teachers take on the market idea of schools as primarily instruments of national economic advancement and are therefore drawn into the punishment culture. Others regard schools as operating for the benefit of the students – an attitude which is far more conducive to their recognising their students as complex individuals with different experiences which have to be acknowledged. Every teacher makes an impact on their students and some even change students' lives. Impact and change can be negative or they can be positive.

Negative impact

Most of the many teachers I have interviewed over the last decade have been committed and dedicated to their students. The negative impact that some of them have had on students stems from their traditional attitude to children and young people, to their own role as teachers, to the purpose of schooling and from their personal values and approach to 'Difference'. Whilst they may be committed, they are inclined towards a pathological view of children and young people and so are oriented towards blaming students or their parents for poor performance or indiscipline in the classroom. They fail to reflect on their own practices and how these might contribute to students' poor behaviour. The survey of Year 10 students mentioned in the last chapter showed clearly that a major cause of conflict between teachers and students is teachers' attitudes to students, and that a major cause of misbehaviour of students is boring lessons. How the teachers expressed their attitudes included shouting at students, public put-downs and humiliation, speaking rudely and showing aggression. For their part, students said that they are less likely to engage in disruptive activities when the lesson is interesting. Discussions with teachers further revealed a systemic problem in the demand that all students take part in all lessons regardless of their particular learning needs. The students who need specialist help are left to flounder, and take out their frustrations on the teacher or other students. These students are victims of an education system which fails to cater adequately for them. But we rationalise their exclusion as 'necessary disciplining'. Clark (1995:24) asserts that,

> Our culture of parenting and pedagogy invariably takes the side of the adult and blames the child for what has been done to him or her... Faced with the power of adults and the social conspiracy of denial, we and our children repress our feelings, idealise or excuse those parents and teachers who abuse us, and tragically, perpetuate the victimisation of the next generation.

The attitude which says that children and young people have to be controlled and punished and all square pegs have to be forced into round holes is disastrous for relationships in schools and certainly for the learning needs of students. Older students in particular will struggle against such control and when they have an underlying suspicion that all this manipulation is 'to turn me from my black identity and impose a white vision of the world', the resistance is that much stronger. By not recognising the specific ways in which groups of children are disadvantaged by schooling structures and processes, we not only deprive ourselves of the opportunity to 'succeed' with these students – we implicate ourselves in their academic failure.

The impact of race

From the time black children enter the education system, they begin to feel the the extent to which their relationships with teachers are mediated by race, even if they cannot articulate it. They are criticised, reprimanded and punished more than other children, as so many researchers have revealed. At times little children are confused and distressed by the blatant racism they experience at the hands of some teachers – the people they look up to, consider infallible, and from whom they seek approval and affirmation.

Sometimes teachers are genuinely well-meaning but do not realise the effects of their practices. When I was an Advisory Teacher, a black couple once complained about racism in their child's school. Their five-year old daughter had reported to her teacher that another child had refused to let her join in a game, telling her it was because 'you are black'. The teacher quite correctly reprimanded the offender and gave the right lesson about valuing everybody and so on. She then took the little black girl on her lap, and in a desire to comfort her declared, 'Anyway, your skin is not black but a beautiful brown'. The child went home that evening and stayed in the bath a long time because, according to her mother, she wanted to 'wash all the dark colour off'. The parents were understandably angry.

The problem that ensued was not because the teacher was racist and had intended to hurt or upset the child. Quite the contrary. She had tried to teach the children the right values *and* to comfort the victim. The real problem was that when the parents complained, she became so defensive and intent on protecting her reputation as a non-racist that it took time, and much pain, not to mention angry exchanges between the school and the parents, before she eventually saw the parents' point of view. However, she reached this point only because the parents had taken the matter up with the school.

What then of the situations, of which there must be many, where the teachers never get to discover the effect of their words or actions on the child, and continuous repetition leaves the child feeling that there is something wrong with her or him. The teacher in question was antiracist in her values. Her intention had been to comfort the little girl and she simply had not thought through what she needed to say to her. What of those situations where the teachers send messages through body language, facial expression, tone of voice, and subtle discriminatory acts, that they do not like the child or that the child does not belong? What of the constant reprimands and scant praise as recorded by Wright (1992 p.19-21). What meaning must school have for students who are constantly subjected to this negative treatment right from the very beginning? Can we be surprised when black students do not reach their expected academic levels? All these questions should form an integral part of teacher preparation and in-service education.

Cullingford *et.al* (1997: 67) assert that:

> ...even if [this is] unintended, teachers can act as a barrier to particular children feeling an accepted part of the school system through subtle forms of bullying that labels, differentiates and excludes.

The teacher who singled out black students in one of the schools I studied, and then told them, *'Don't ask me for an explanation. I don't have to give you an explanation. I am a teacher and when I ask to see your diaries you give them to me'*, epitomises the Victorian attitude to children and also to race, which students (especially at secondary school) resent so deeply. His was an unnecessary display of power which seemed, at least to the boys, to be motivated by racism. It may be that he felt he had to establish his authority because he thought it would be challenged by these particular students. However, amongst the greatest causes of conflict with students is the power struggle some teachers engage in. Students will be drawn into such struggles if they feel they are being treated unjustly.

The Brazilian philosopher and educator Paulo Freire taught that the most effective teaching is achieved when the teacher shares knowledge with and is able to learn from students rather than assuming a position of absolute authority over them. This is not to be confused with teachers abdicating responsibility for control in the classroom. Students generally appreciate an ordered and undisrupted lesson. What I am talking about are teachers who abuse their position in order to gain control. This abuse can take the form of over-disciplining or picking on black students because such teachers feel they do not understand them, or expect trouble from them.

On the other hand, when teachers feel insecure about reprimanding black students because they are afraid of being accused of racism, and fail to do so when it is warranted, they provoke equally detrimental results. Generally these are teachers who need help and re-skilling. In Catholic School, Ms Christian created space for teachers to meet and informally discuss what constituted fair treatment and what it was that all students, black and white, expected from teachers. Such openness provided the opportunity to explain, for example, that

> If a (black) pupil has behaved badly, they must be referred. *Pupils expect that* (my emphasis) because they know if they are being reprimanded unfairly or if they are being reprimanded because the teacher cares about them.

Ms Christian believes that black students do not respond any differently from other students *unless* they feel that they are being treated unfairly.

Teacher orientation

The question of the teacher's personal position on or attitude to discipline and to students in general is particularly important given the relationship between exclusion and the prison system discussed earlier.

Although it would be difficult without the statistical evidence to draw a direct relationship between an *individual's* ideological orientation and the *actual exclusion* (permanent or fixed) of a student from school, one can with some confidence contend that ideologies, or values and beliefs, have a direct effect on the exclusion or inclusion of students from equal participation in schooling. One can assume this in a general sense because in all the cases of exclusion I examined in the various studies, the number of referrals (that is, written reports of poor or disruptive behaviour) by the classroom teacher was generally crucial in deciding whether the student should be temporarily excluded, while the number of fixed exclusions were, in all cases, taken into account for deciding a permanent exclusion. The teachers' ideological orientation – the extent to which they took upon themselves the responsibility for student behaviour – was likely to determine the number of referrals of students the teachers would make. Equally, any teacher's racialised perspectives were likely to affect the outcomes for black and other minority group students.

The following is an example of the kind of orientation which can have negative effects on black students. This is from a shire school with only 3% black students but where black students represented 25% of all exclusions. In a discussion with two of the teachers, Mrs Willis and Mrs Quinn, I enquired about specific students whose progress I was tracking. They taught three of these students, but could only talk about two of them as the third was a persistent truant whom they had scarcely seen. These teachers illustrate what I mean by ideological orientation in their discourses about black students. It will be seen in the example below, that Mrs Quinn goes from the specific to the broader category of black students without any prompting on my part.

MB. What kind of progress would you say Gavin was making?

Mrs Willis. Very little. Very little. He and Sean are grossly underachieving. Which is sad really because they are both quite intelligent boys.

MB. Why do you suppose they are not making any progress?

Mrs Quinn. If you ask me, and I'm sorry that I've got to say it, I think they have a real problem about their colour. I think that's a real problem with our black pupils. I find it inconceivable that a teacher would deliberately single out a pupil because of their colour. I think some-

105

thing happens to the Afro-Caribbean children when they get to the second or third year. If you start talking to some of them, there is an underlying chip on the shoulder. And yet it's not because of their race that they are picked on. It's because they become so laid back. They stop trying. I don't know what it is about them that they take things so easy.

Mrs Willis. We all have off days, children have off days, it's not just Afro-Caribbean children. It's the underachieving that bothers me.

Mrs Quinn. Oh as people, they are super, or can be. They have such outgoing personalities.

Mrs Willis. But do you think that's general, because there's Nigel who said, 'I've worked hard in years 1 and 2, and I've decided that I'm not working anymore'. He's English, British.

Mrs Quinn. That's if you look at it on an individual basis. But there's something... I'm sure something happens to some of them which may lie dormant and they may try to sweep it under the carpet for so long, and then it comes to the fore. It's this colour difference. I never seem to notice it in any other backgrounds...It seems such a shame to feel that different colours should have any effect on any of us because there is beauty in all peoples, whether they are Japanese or Chinese, all the different colours.

One can see how Mrs Willis tries to cling to a notion of diversity which is not bound by colour, whereas Mrs Quinn, despite her protestations about beauty in all peoples, seems sure that colour is largely the reason why black students act in particular ways, thus cancelling out or at any rate reducing the possibility of viewing each of them as an individual. There is no desire on her part to harm black students and she seemed genuinely concerned about 'underachieve-ment'. But, equally, she shows little understanding of the ways in which people's experiences are mediated by disability, racism, sexism, homophobia, and other disabling practices.

In his study of Kilby School, Mac an Ghaill (1988) described as 'crude caricatures' the racist stereotypes held of black students. He noted how African Caribbean students were generally judged in be-havioural and not academic terms, unlike the South Asian students.

The example above supports the findings of Mac an Ghaill but also underscores the biological basis on which some teachers interpret the behaviour of black students. Mrs Quinn illustrates the use of 'racial frames of reference' (Figueroa, 1991) to assign particular characteristics to whole groups of students, even in the face of individuals who defy the stereotype. Conversely, the group stereotype could be used to make assumptions about individual behaviour. Mrs Quinn again:

> **MB**. Do you teach Glenda?
>
> **Mrs Quinn**. I don't actually teach her. I bump into her in the corridor. She's very pleasant, but I imagine as soon as you get her into a situation where you want her to work, there could be a lot of conflict. I think she's very, I think she's got a chip on her shoulder. She's never accused me of picking on her, but I could imagine that's what she would do. She's got a kind of glare in her eyes of animosity.

That this student has been written off as a result, probably, of staffroom talk is evident from the authoritative way in which Mrs Quinn, *with no personal knowledge*, assumes what Glenda is likely to do. The 'chip on the shoulder', which Mac an Ghaill also found to be one of the ways in which teachers typified the black students, is thus less an individual characteristic of the student, and more a function of 'truth' about black people to which Mrs Quinn evidently subscribes, as revealed when she said that black students had a problem with colour. She is unaware of the contradiction in her statement when she describes the student first as very pleasant and then as having 'a glare in her eyes of animosity'.

Contradiction is one of the hallmarks of the stereotype and racial myth. One contradiction operates when black students are seen *as a group to naturally* behave in certain ways but are nevertheless expected to behave as individuals. There is little recognition of the tension created for black students by being expected to behave as individuals while being judged and assessed as a group. Examining the contradictions and the inconsistencies in their own thoughts and statements is one way teachers could gain better understanding of how stereotypes operate against particular groups.

Positive impact

After several studies of the pedagogic practices of teachers Haberman (1995) concluded that there were certain characteristics which made some teachers successful with 'children in poverty' or children in inner city schools, most of whom were African American or Latino. He called these 'star' teachers. Similarly, in her study of schools, Gloria Ladson-Billings (1994) identified teachers who she found to be particularly effective with African American students. Some of the characteristics these researchers identified in these teachers were that they made it their business to get to know their students and communities. They found out the things that mattered to the students, the issues that affected their lives, and they taught the normal curriculum by drawing on the lives and experiences of their students and thus making their teaching relevant and interesting to them.

During my study of a primary school in one London borough, two black teachers talked about the usefulness of knowing and being part of the communities from which the children came. They were able to relate to the children both formally, in school, and informally at local events at which they met the children and their families. They also felt that as black teachers they had an influential role in the lives of black students in that they could help them relate certain behaviours and attitudes to issues of identity and self-respect. This is not an impossible task for white teachers too, as Ladson-Billings found with white teachers who were successful with minority group students. But the requirement for white teachers to want to get to know the students, to become familiar with and empathetic towards their concerns, to believe in them as people with potential whose experiences are mediated by racialised structures which have profound effects on their lives. They must be willing to loosen the hold, if not give up altogether, and to confront some firmly held but damaging beliefs.

Our Ms Christian did just this. Although she did not live in the local area, she went out into the black community and made contact with community leaders; she listened to people's experiences, tried to understand some of the political perspectives of black people, created space for black parents to air their concerns in the school; and she was able to build the trust and confidence of her students. There were other white teachers in her school who were popular with black students because they believed in the students and related to them as people and not as socially constructed misfits. I have met teachers who related equally well with Gypsy Traveller students, with students from refugee and asylum-seeking families, and with South Asian students.

In the matter of student behaviour, Haberman (1995) argues that discipline is not a priority for 'star' teachers because they see problems as part of their job. He compares them to dentists who, he says, 'are not floored when a patient's open mouth reveals diseased gums or decayed teeth...They assume problems are the reason for needing skilled practitioners' (p.4).

Haberman's successful teachers saw poor student behaviour not as extraneous to the task of teaching but as part and parcel of it. Students, in all their diversity and for all the challenges they presented, were the reason they became teachers. So they took responsibility for students' behaviour, using their organisational and pedagogic skills to keep them learning and engaged, so that discipline was not a major issue. They found ways of engaging even the most difficult of students, recognising that each is unique and brings with them a unique set of problems as well as talents and interests.

Although I did not go out to find 'star' teachers in my studies, I encountered several examples of students who were considered by some teachers to be difficult but who other teachers managed to inspire and engage in ways which brought out the best in them. I discussed the same Glenda whom Mrs Quinn described as having 'a glare in her eyes' with another teacher who had a good relationship with her, and it was apparent that the reason for this lay in the teacher's general orientation and attitude to students.

Ms Steyn: It all hinged on a book which we were reading in class which used the word 'nigger' quite a lot. She refused to take part in lessons and became quite aggressive. And that's how everyone would see her, as this aggressive black kid. There is an inability for a lot of people to see that aggression is well-founded. People don't see that people don't become aggressive without good reason and that it isn't enough for us to say, 'Oh, aggressive child'. You've actually got to take on board why the child is aggressive. Anyway, I talked to her quite a lot. She had called me a racist and I found that very upsetting. I had never been called this before. *But I think it's up to us to provide the environment where Glenda and people like her feel safe, and if we are not providing that environment, we can't be surprised if they are aggressive* (my emphasis). It isn't enough to say, 'Well, I'm not a racist'. Well, maybe we're not, but as a white woman in the teaching profession, I have to take the responsibility for that. I have an obligation to handle this in a certain way. It's a hard fight to win.

Ms Steyn clearly recognises that people are positioned differently in society and will resist the practices they find oppressive. But she also believes that schools have a professional obligation to acknowledge these societal differences if they are to cater equally for all their students. She regards ignoring the different experiences of students and treating all students 'the same' less as deliberate racism than as benign neglect. Her views did not preclude the possibility of some staff being blatantly racist and as being partly responsible for a general deterioration in the efforts made by the black students in their school work and their relations with others. This teacher saved Glenda from expulsion. As Glenda herself declared, 'If it hadn't been for Ms Steyn, I would have been chucked out of school and probably be pushing a baby's pram by now'. Glenda's relationship with this teacher changed her attitude to school and she was able to stay on and pass her GCSEs.

Teacher expectations

An indication of the ideological orientation of certain teachers towards students can be found in general class-based statements such as 'the kinds of children who come to this school wouldn't appreciate that', or 'they wouldn't be able to cope with that', or 'you can't really expect that kind of achievement from the children who come to this school'. In one school such attitudes created a vicious cycle in which low expectations led to student boredom and deteriorating behaviour. The school consequently became tougher on discipline so as not to lose the middle class students and perhaps damage the school's academic profile. Low teacher expectations were a problem for all working class students, but expectations were also racialised, thus compounding the situation for black students. Yet even here some of the teachers managed to have a positive impact on their students. A teacher admired by many of the students said this of the school:

> When I first came here, I told the children they must try to get As, Bs, and Cs. That is a pre-requisite for getting into higher education. If you have got lower than that, you can still go for higher education but you have to re-sit or do an access course. The Head of English came to me and said, 'Mr Davey, I understand you are telling the children that D, E, F, and G are not good grades'. I said, 'I tell them that these are not the grades to aim for'. And he turned to me and he told me, I even wrote it down, he said, 'Mr Davey, the children you want to teach don't come to this school. They do not come to this school'. He meant any children, white or black, but the majority of the children in the class were black. Well, I had sixteen children in the class and thirteen out of the sixteen, seven blacks and six whites, got A, B, and C. He was shocked, he was stunned....They think children who come from this area can't pass literature. I had twenty-three children in my (literature) class, and twenty got A, B, and C ...I am not saying it to boast. I am saying it because if I can do it in the same school, *the same school* (original emphasis) then they can do it as well.

Mr Davey epitomises the 'good' teacher in his strong belief that the problems students face are systemic, and that it is up to the individual teacher not to support such a system. Both Haberman (1995) and Ladson-Billings (1994) found that effective teachers tended to work in *opposition* to a status quo they saw as operating against the interests of students. A major problem in the school above was the institutionalised low expectations held by staff and how these worked against the interests of students. Mr Davey believed that if teachers lower their expectations they will make less effort with the students. But he himself made a positive impact on the students he taught, some of whom went on to higher education – a rare occurrence in this school.

Mr Davey placed the onus of responsibility for student outcomes on individual class teachers and on the school itself. Students talked about how much time he took to help them understand ideas and information, how they felt that he really cared about their success, how easily he kept order in the classroom while still having a laugh with them. Instead of learning from Mr Davey, the Head of Department criticised him for raising the students' expectations of their own abilities. This can be contrasted with Ms Christian, who praised staff in her school for skills and talents of this kind which, she believed, needed to be shared. She said

> What we do in school is to ask staff to highlight their good practice. We look at Jim's group and say if Jim can get 83% A-Cs, why can't everybody get 83% A-Cs, because Jim is teaching the same group as everybody else. So what do you do Jim? Alison, you get good results, what do you do? I highlight them and say, You tell the rest of the staff what you do. Then the other staff look at what is preventing them from getting similar results.

Conclusion

The aim of this chapter has been to illustrate the role played by teachers and schools in affecting the life chances of their students.

For my analytical framework, I adopted the theories of educationists whose studies of teachers and teaching have led them to conclude that it is the teacher's own organisational styles and content presentation which determine the extent to which students remain sufficiently engaged not to present a disciplinary challenge in the classroom. They argue that teachers who do not reflect on their own teaching methodologies and who transfer the blame onto the students, their families or certain external factors to explain their behaviour, are more likely to create situations where disciplining students becomes necessary. When teachers also operate with a racialised frame of reference, we see how their ideological orientation is likely to precipitate a level of sanctions on black students which is unwarranted by their behaviour.

The contemporary context of teaching might make it more or less difficult for teachers to maintain the high ideals set out by educationists such as Haberman (1995) or Ladson-Billings (1994). The requirements of a national curriculum, for example, restrict the opportunities for teachers to make teaching culturally relevant to students from all ethnic groups. Furthermore, the existence of school league tables and market principles, and the removal of many of the resources upon which schools depended to support students, has de-skilled and disempowered teachers. Fine (1991, p.140) sums it up:

> Disempowered teachers are unlikely to create democratic communities inside their classrooms, but are more likely to move toward silencing. Disempowered teachers are unlikely to view the 'personal problems' of students as their professional responsibility, but are more likely to render them outside the domain of education. And disempowered teachers are unlikely to create academic contexts of possibility and transformation, but are more likely to want to retire (early).

Despite this context, and accepting that teachers cannot fully support their students effectively in such conditions, the teachers' orientation can clearly make a significant difference to the educational experience of their students. Reflecting honestly on one's own abilities and limitations, questioning one's own attitudes to the students overall and to the individuals one teaches, viewing each as a unique creation who requires a sometimes challenging but always compassionate approach, giving one's utmost to the students and being prepared at times to challenge an ethos and system which goes against the interests of students – these are what make the difference to students' learning. Even in environments in which students experience education negatively, there are individual teachers who manage to inspire and motivate students whom other teachers consider difficult.

The effective teachers were used in some schools as resources for in-service education. The idea of collaborative work among teachers could be extended to a notion of mentoring, whereby teachers who experience difficulties are helped and supported by those who do not face such problems. In one school, the Head of Department was overall mentor of the teachers in that department, developing an approach to the students, to teaching, setting homework and marking it, tracking and monitoring students, sanctions and rewards, which was agreed by the whole department and followed through in a consistent manner. Teachers discussed their progress in regular departmental meetings and met individually with the Head of Department to discuss student progress and identify any support they themselves might need.

The issue of effective teaching comes back to the ethos of the school, the support and leadership offered by the headteacher, the teamwork, collaborative and supportive work between teachers, and the school having a 'We' rather than a 'Them and Us' culture. In other words, where there is a sense of community between students and staff all teachers can have a positive impact on their students.

7

Parents' perspectives

In writings about race and education, black parents' voices are seldom heard. Yet it is parents who have been the prime movers in the attempts to secure better educational opportunities for their children (Chevannes and Reeves, 1987). Black parents' concerns about the over-representation of their children in exclusions goes back a long way, at least to the late 1960s.

In *The Heart of the Race*, Bryan, Dadzie and Scafe (1984) describe black parents' sense of powerlessness to do anything about the racism and discrimination their children faced in schools. There was a sense in which the new arrivals – as they were at the time – felt like 'guests', with limited rights. And they believed that school was the domain of the professional, set beyond a boundary that parents could not cross. But as evidence steadily accumulated of the high levels of intolerance and discrimination, and the low levels of academic achievement their children experienced (Coard, 1971) it became clear that something had to be done.

Coard provided the spur for the development and growth of Supplementary or Saturday Schools, where black children could receive extra academic support from members of their own communities and be insulated from the racism they encountered at school from their teachers and peers. Parents I interviewed talked about their own experiences of schooling and how this affected their ability to support their children. Elbeda, who in the 1960s had gone to the same school her children now attended, remembered the defining moment which led to a downward spiral in her academic performance:

Elbeda: I came from the Caribbean at the age of 12, so I went straight into secondary school. We had been given very structured teaching in my school in Jamaica and we knew our times tables and knew how to do long divisions, you know, and I was quite good at arithmetic. I remember one day the teacher gave us all several pages of arithmetic to do and said that as soon as we had finished we should let her know so she could check what we had done. I remember I was amazed by how easy the sums were. It was stuff I had done at my school in Jamaica. Anyway, I was the first to finish and I was going up to her desk when she said to me really rudely, 'Sit down. You can't possibly have finished yet'. So I said I had finished. She took my book, checked my sums and then turned to the class and said, 'What do we do to people who cheat?' No-one said anything so she said to me, 'I want you to show me where you copied these answers from. I will not have cheats in my class', and she tore the pages out of the book, told me to sit down next to her and do them again. I was so humiliated and so scared that of course I didn't get very far with them which just confirmed to her that I must have cheated the first time. That was a real lesson for me because I made up my mind that I was never going to expose myself like that again. Most of the time I was bored, but I would never put my hands up if I knew the answer. I was put into low streams, in fact there were only four black children in the school and we were all put into low streams for all our subjects. I left school with only two CSEs. Our parents just didn't know how to help us. And to think that my children are going through more of the same, but different if you see what I mean...

Painful personal experiences of this kind produced varied responses from parents. Elbeda talked about her feelings that she had let her children down by allowing these early experiences to intimidate and paralyse her and being afraid of going into school to support her children. Other parents were moved to go to the school whenever their children reported unfairness or discrimination, so became labelled as 'aggressive' and 'volatile' (see Mac an Ghaill, 1994).

Jennifer: I had such bad experiences when I was at school and my parents really weren't there for me because they had so much to face themselves. Anyway I decided that I was not going to let my children go through the same thing. And it's not like I was there every day of every week, but when they started sending him home for such minor things, I just thought I couldn't let them get away with destroying my child's chances. So I used to go to the school and the headmaster was always very nice to me. But it was always the same teacher, and I think in the end they excluded (my son) not because he had done anything so wrong, but because they didn't want to have to deal with me any-more.

'Partnerships' between parents and schools are considered important for children's education. But such relationships are rarely partner-ships in the sense that parents share an equal position with teachers in determining what happens to children at school. One teacher said,

In my mind, teachers expect parents to come here just for the parents' evening, the disciplining... I think that teachers expect parents to support the school when it suits the teachers for the parents to support the school. But if the parents come in about something that they want, then it's like, 'This is our school and parents should not be involved in that'.

The term partnership, it seems, is merely a rhetorical device which presents schools as open and willing to work with parents in the interests of the students while masking the power the school has to ensure that parents comply with its non-negotiated mechanisms for imposing discipline. Tomlinson (1984) contends that:

Schools are not in any case flexible in their response to parents, partly because a liberal stance prefers not to single out particular groups of parents for particular treatment, and partly because lack of knowledge and poor communication may inhibit teachers from understanding minority community needs and wishes (p.10)

What emerges from the accounts by black parents is that despite teachers adopting a liberal stance, they have generally singled out black parents for particular treatment by allowing stereotypes of black people to inform their relations with black families (Mac an Ghaill, 1994). Jennifer's experience, which was by no means ex-ceptional, shows black parents inhabiting a contradictory space bet-ween being labelled uninterested in their child's education because they do not go into school, and being labelled aggressive and uncooperative if they attend and venture any criticism of the school. Parents endorsed many of the points raised by the black students. All across the wide range of schools involved and the varied locations of those interviewed, parents' responses to the issue of exclusions were consistent. They were interviewed separately from their children but were wholly in agreement with them and had equally strong feelings about the issues. Like their children, none of the parents tried to justify bad behaviour or to pretend that their children's behaviour was always beyond reproach. Again, it was the selective nature of the censure, or the inconsistency with which sanctions were applied, that disturbed them. Of the eighteen parents interviewed, only one couple were in complete agreement with the school about the reasons for and process of their child's exclusion.

How parents see relationships between students and teachers

Parents thought that teachers' attitudes significantly damaged features of their relationships with black students and were a prime factor in the over-representation of black students in exclusions. Parents supported the students' beliefs that teachers treated them with little respect, did not listen to their views and allowed racial stereotypes to influence their opinions. Parents felt that teachers, as the educators, should be the ones who provide the parameters which guide student behaviour – that they should, in other words, be role models to the students.

> **Mavis:** They don't show the children respect. They shout at them, put them down and basically don't talk to them like to another human being. Yet they expect the children to be saying, 'Yes Sir, Yes Miss' all the time.

Here again is evidence that teachers talk to students in ways regarded in some schools as routine but which black parents – like the students – find disrespectful. Some parents advised their children not to retaliate when they felt the teachers did not show them respect. They tried to instil in their children the notion of conforming to the school's demands as a way of beating them at their own game, insisting that they be punctual, dress neatly and be respectful.

Jacqui: I tried to say to him, 'Just ignore them. They are not going to be there in the future when you are looking for a job. Don't cheek them back, you know, you're the only one that's going to lose out, but it's useless asking our children to do that when the very people who are supposed to be in charge of their welfare treat them with so little respect.

Teachers would approve such conformity. And there is evidence to show that black students are the least likely to truant (Schools Exclusion Unit 1998) and the most likely group to come to school clean and well dressed. The kind of disrespect teachers showed students seems to bear no relation to school uniform, or to whether children came to school properly equipped (a problem presented by students from all ethnic groups). The parents were as well aware of the preconceptions white teachers in general have about black people as the black teachers and students were. The parents believed that these unfounded preconceptions led teachers to assume that black students were more likely than other students to engage in certain types of behaviour and consequently to pick on them unjustly.

Liz: Apparently a supply teacher walked into the classroom and there was a group of boys in the corner who were messing about and didn't pay attention when they were told to sit down. She went and called the Head of Year and said that the black boy was the main culprit. He had to go to the office and of course he wouldn't tell the Head who the others were, so he got suspended, and he wasn't even the main person involved. When the other boys realised that he was being suspended, they went and gave themselves up. She'd only picked him out because she didn't know their names, you know, and he stood out from the crowd.

Liz's story provides an interesting example of racial discrimination – one that illuminates one of the many reasons why black students are over-represented in exclusions. The supply teacher may not have been motivated by malice against black people, but one has to ask what she would have done had there been no black students in the class. It is not unknown for teachers to detain a whole class, or in this case, perhaps, all the boys rather than allow one boy to pay the penalty simply because his colour made him stand out from the rest.

It may have been convenient for the teacher, but what about the implications for the student?

One of the side effects of getting picked on was that students became labelled as trouble-makers and found it difficult to shake off this image. It even followed them to a new school, so they could not make a fresh start. In the study carried out for Barnardos and the Family Services Unit, a parent I interviewed underlined this point.

> **Brenda:** He seems to settle down and he can have good times, and then it'll just, I don't know, he seems to get one teacher that says, 'We know all about you', and it starts all over again.

I wrote in that study that:

> This labelling did not stop with the pupil in question but was extended to his/her siblings which tended to establish a 'family' rather than an individual reputation, with unfortunate consequences. One parent said,

> 'She compares my two daughters to him all the time. She pulls them all the time in the corridor about his behaviour – so now, both of them, it's no longer – they're in school – but it's 'Can I have a day off?' and 'I don't feel well', and it's because they know she's going to teach them and she's going to compare them all the time and it's not right'.

Parents also reported that teachers do not listen to what students have to say so they can give them a fair hearing and avoid making unfair decisions. The students themselves persistently made complaints about the failure of teachers to listen to them. Both parents and students thought that if teachers listened more to what the students said, they might become more aware of the causes of the conflict involving black students – for example, how much racist name-calling and racial harassment they endured (see CRE, 1997). Both the CRE and the Runnymede Trust specifically recommended to the DfEE that this problem be made explicit in the government's so-called 'Six Pack' (DfEE 1999) which gave guidelines to schools on a number of issues relating to exclusion. Parents felt strongly that this failure by teachers to listen to the students left students feeling unsupported and uncared for in school. Although this is not an issue for black students alone, the perception that teachers were more likely to blame the black students heightened the sense of grievance that decisions were racially biased instead of objective and fair. The sense of grievance felt by the black parents and their children was directed less against the students who were racially abusive than against the teachers and other adults in positions of responsibility, for their failure to take a firm stand on racist abuse, or professing concern and doing nothing.

> **Rosina:** She just wouldn't listen to what Andrea had to say. She heard what the other girl had to say, and that was that, you know, just not caring that there are two sides to every story. Andrea just felt that she had no-one to turn to, and I can't blame her for feeling so rebellious. She just felt that she was facing a brick wall. She was doing so well, you know, and this is what they've done to her.

Although the parents' accounts of their children's experiences are at second hand, there is such consistency in the reports that they cannot be dismissed. My studies were carried out in various cities such as Bristol, Leeds, Manchester, and different parts of London. White parents of black children were also involved. The Barnardos/FSU study (Cohen *et.al* 1994), in which Cohen interviewed a group of white parents in relation to their (white) children who had been expelled, reinforced the power of class in influencing teachers' relations with parents. Interestingly, the racialised nature of teachers' relations with the white mothers of black children gave these parents a qualitatively different experience from other white parents, as I discuss below.

Teacher-parent relationships

A strong theme to emerge out of the analysis of parents' views of their relations with teachers was their feelings of powerlessness and lack of control when their children were excluded. They echoed the students' complaints that teachers and others in authority did not listen to them or heed their concerns. In the Barnardos/FSU study I wrote the following:

> The sense of powerlessness was compounded for the parents by the feeling of alienation from official discourse and the inconsistency of the support (if any) which they received or had been promised by the

local education office. Officials were said to backtrack on their promises, or to make offers of help which they never followed up, to give
up help when a parent or child most needed it, or simply not to communicate with the parents about whatever progress was being made
regarding their child's education. There was a sense of hopelessness
because of lack of access to information which would help them to be
less dependent on others to get things done (p.52).

Brown (1998) affirms that the power relationship between professionals and parents not of the professional class is deeply uneven and
that this imbalance can cause the skills of parents to be devalued by
teachers and other professionals. Mac an Ghaill (1994), too, points
to 'a failure to acknowledge the differential positioning of parents to
schooling and its discourses of social exclusion' (p.161). These
writers believe that a major obstacle to good relations between
schools and minority ethnic group parents and their communities
lies in the preconceptions and racial or ethnic stereotypes held by
teachers. Tomlinson (1984:198) states that:

one way of improving home-school relations with ethnic minority
parents would be the introduction of much more structured links,
both to inform parents about the education system in general and
thus help make the education of their own children more meaningful,
and also to encourage teachers to listen to the views of ethnic
minority parents without preconceived stereotyping.

Parents identified stereotyping as a major cause of the poor relations
between many black working class parents and schools. There was,
for example, the persistent stereotype that black parents are not
interested in their children's education or academic progress (Brown,
1998). Tomlinson (1984, p.15) adds that:

the research caricature of the low-achieving working class child and
his or her low level of parental encouragement may have had more
effect on teachers than is generally acknowledged... (Yet) the stereotype of the apathetic, uninterested parent is not supported by
research.

Most of the black parents I interviewed had attended school in
Britain. They believed that the persistence of the stereotype of the

aggressive African-Caribbean parent was used by teachers as an excuse for not paying attention to what black parents were saying and therefore as a way of avoiding having to cater for the needs of black children.

In the study commissioned by Barnardos and the Family Service Units, (1994) Cohen interviewed the white parents and I the black parents. We found several parallels between the experiences of white parents and black. Both ethnic groups reported experiences of powerlessness and being treated as a nobody. However, the black parents did not always accept that their children caused difficulties of a severity that merited temporary or permanent exclusion. Whereas the white parents generally accepted that their children were indeed difficult or had problems requiring specialist help, the black parents were often baffled by reports of behaviour which seemed to be out of character for the child concerned. The white parents felt that they needed access to information about their rights, access to the people who made decisions about their children, adequate and appropriate facilities for the children who needed specialist help, and to be treated with dignity and respect. The black parents also felt they needed support of this kind, but they also wanted the cessation of the racist assumptions which often led to unfair treatment of themselves and their children. They resented, for example, the assumption that black people were alien, had lower standards, that these standards were imported into Britain and contaminated British schools and, by extension, British (read white) children.

Jennifer: The teacher said, 'We just don't accept that kind of behaviour in this country', you know, treating me like I was an immigrant when I was born and brought up in this country. And in fact, my experiences in school were *so* (original emphasis) bad, I'd never have experienced that kind of thing in Jamaica. So trying to make out like countries where black people come from the children behave badly – and it's exactly the opposite.

My studies also revealed that the feeling of being stereotyped was shared by the white parents of black children. One, a teacher, was convinced that half the problems her son faced arose because he was

123

black. She described her first meeting with the headteacher of the school:

> I was called to a meeting by the headteacher, and when I walked into his office, his jaw dropped. He was visibly shocked. He just hadn't expected a white middle-class woman and one in his own profession!

Whilst the fact that she was a middle class white parent of a black child caused the headteacher to react with shock, working class white parents were reported to be met with contempt.

> **Avril:** Because my two older children are half-caste because my first husband was black, they just think I'm trash, and they take it out on all my children, even the white ones. I'm sure that's why my daughter and my son had so much trouble at school.

> **Patricia:** I'm sure Rachel's father being black has something to do with the kind of help I've had. The last headmistress just didn't hide the fact that she held me in contempt.

Working class parents, black and white, generally felt that the teachers and other professionals they had to deal with over their children's exclusions did not respect them. Associated with the sense of powerlessness and lack of control over their own and their children's lives, was a sense that officialdom or the (white) middle class world of schools and staffrooms treated them in a manner intended to cause misunderstanding and conflict and close off opportunities for proper communication. There were strong echoes of students' accounts in their statements, re-inforcing the argument that parents, in particular working class parents, are differentially positioned in the school system and that systemic practices inhibit their attempts to create partnerships with the teachers.

One parent said she became so fed up with constant requests for her to visit the school, that she decided voluntarily to move her son to another school. She told me that it didn't matter whether or not he was in school if something bad happened – his involvement was assumed or he was bound to be questioned about it. He had begun so well, she said, until he had questioned his history teacher about his disconnection of Egypt from Africa, and things began to go downhill. Then his behaviour began to deteriorate, but she was sure this was because the history teacher provoked him with constant put-downs and he felt compelled to retaliate. Since he had moved to a school which took a preventive approach to discipline, her son was a 'new person' and his academic performance had burgeoned. An important element of this school's preventive approach was its policy of listening to and respecting students' views.

Another parent talked about the significant role of the headteacher in fostering good relations with parents. The headteacher at his son's school was well respected by black parents because of her efforts to get to know the families of her students and understand their various concerns. He said:

> She developed the pastoral support so well that parents are able to come and talk to her about their children getting arrested or getting into trouble outside the school. Parents have the confidence to come to her as a friend – she is seen as a friend in arms, struggling together with them for the good of their children. The school has been able to win the confidence of the parents to say that we are all working together for the success of the child.

Conclusion

From interviews with parents, it appears that class is an important determinant of the quality of relationships between parents and teachers. The interaction of race, class and gender adds another dimension to the relations between schools and black parents. According to parents, this goes some way to explaining why black students are more likely to be excluded.

Black parents confirmed many of the issues black students identified as contributing to their over-representation in exclusions. Some of these issues were echoed in the relationships between schools and parents. Despite the current rhetoric about home-school partnerships, it seems that working class parents in particular do not share with the school the power to determine the academic futures of their children. Parents communicated a sense of hopelessness about the decisions that were taken about their children. They felt powerless to influence the outcomes when relations broke down between their children and the school, and indeed felt still more excluded or obliged to comply with whatever the school decided.

Many of the difficulties faced by black students were said to lie in discriminatory or unfair practices. Parents identified prevailing stereotypes of black people as influencing teachers in their dealings with black students. Such stereotypes also influenced the teachers' relationships with the parents, rendering them conflictual rather than friendly or productive. The losers in these situations were inevitably the students.

The responsibility for creating proper structures of communication between home and school lies with the school. The lack of such structures for communicating effectively with black parents must, in situations where communication is generally experienced as being mediated by racism, be a serious obstacle to black students' education. According to parents, it increases the chances of exclusion and exacerbates the long term consequences for their futures.

Many schools do try to improve communication with minority ethnic group parents. They take into account the need for interpreters or translators if parents need language support; they try to arrange meetings at times which suit the cultural or life-style needs of different groups; they send letters home written in both English and the community language; they seek help from local community organisations, whether social, academic or religious, including Mediation Services; they employ Liaison Officers and they create space and time in their school for black or other parental groups to meet and discuss and share issues with the school.

Parents will often approach problems in school with hostility because they have never had the assurance that the school is on their and their children's side. They, too, experience schools as a culture of 'Them and Us'. One headteacher decided to provide an information service for the many South Asian parents of children at his school, so held a series of meetings in the community and not in the school, at a time that was convenient for most parents and mainly the mothers, with interpreters present. This was met with astonishment by the parents that the school cared about them and their needs. But after these initiatives the community, which had barely known its school, tried to work with and support it in any way they could.

Black parents also have a role in building good relationships with their children's school. By and large teachers felt that parents were co-operative and supportive, but that they needed to play a greater part in supervising their children's homework, especially at secondary level. There was concern that some students, especially the boys, stayed out too late and were tired next morning. Teachers also felt that parents needed to be more aware of the pressures exerted by the peer group and to realise that their children's behaviour at school might be different from their behaviour at home. Establishing such understandings could help schools and parents to agree specific strategies for helping and supporting the children.

Clearly, parents will have to play their part by making sure that their children meet the academic and behaviour expectations of the school. But for parents and school to work together, the onus is on the school to ensure that the door is genuinely open. Parents must feel that the school values their input; that they are welcome; that their concerns are taken seriously and that the teachers are willing to listen and act on their concerns.

8
Conclusion

Summary

We have come to a point where we accept the exclusion of students from school as normal. This is surely a backward step for society, not just for the students affected. Society has a responsibility to address the problem from as many angles as possible and with some urgency. The evidence suggests that it is currently approached from an alarmingly limited range of perspectives, coming from government, teaching unions and teachers. There are few signs that the views and concerns of students and their parents are taken into account.

In this concluding chapter I suggest approaches which place students at the centre of the decisions taken in schools. It should be possible to provide an education which appears relevant to students, gains qualifications for them and is conducted within the parameters of a national curriculum. But an education which has relevance for students requires us to re-orient our thinking about and attitudes towards children and young people, even if we have to overturn some of our cherished beliefs. It is adults who have the responsibility to create a society in which children and young people want and are able to learn and an environment in which students feel safe to learn – safe from racist, sexist, homophobic and other abuse and social injustice.

We have all the information we need to help us in this process. Numerous studies of schools and education have shown the various ways in which the education system creates winners and losers. Some sociologists of education have argued that the processes of schooling play an important part in helping to regulate national and international economies (Young, 1971; Sharp and Green, 1975; Bowles and Gintis, 1976; Ball, 1987; Apple, 1990). Students' life chances, they argue, are limited or enhanced so as to position them, through employment, according to the needs of capital. The allocative role of schools is achieved through processes and procedures which reflect middle class interests and therefore favour the students who already possess the cultural capital required to succeed academically. The sifting process by schools operates largely on the basis of which group each student belongs to.

Writers such as Ball (1987) argue against the tendency to draw a direct conspiratorial relationship between the activities of schools and the needs of capital. They see the relationship rather as a complex arrangement which does not necessarily require the tacit or conspiratorial agreement of those who work in schools. Vested interests, they argue, are maintained through discourses which reflect dominant groups in society. As a result of their failure to reflect the diverse interests of the social groups who have little access to the structures of power, schools inevitably support the status quo – a status quo which correlates with structures of economic power.

The notion of excluding students from school has been discussed here within this context. The processes of exclusion describe not only the overt practices which remove a student from the physical boundaries of the school but embrace also a range of subtle and covert practices, deliberate or unconscious, which exclude the individual both emotionally and psychologically. These processes have been clearly identified in all the research projects described.

Labelling

Labelling allows for the construction of particular groups as 'deviant' (Becker, 1963). Students can have their access to knowledge impeded by the assumptions held by teachers about the class/cultural group to which each is perceived to belong (Keddie, 1984). These assumptions do not necessarily signal a teacher's deliberate intentions but they do reflect certain social and cultural values based on historic stereotypes.

Alongside the negative construction of certain groups is the cultural imaging of children – this is a more general form of labelling but it, too, has implications for children's educational provision. The assumptions about children, like those about particular groups, penetrate the taken-for-granted or normative aspects of a school's activities and translate into practices which allocate certain groups predominantly to a particular quality or type of service. Several writers have provided examples of these processes and how they result in unequal treatment of students (Keddie 1984; McLaren, 1986; Wright *et.al* (2000). Other studies have shown how students are allocated to particular subject bands, sets and streams on the basis of their class or ethnicity rather than their performance and differential education provided accordingly (Oakes, 1985; Wright, 1987).

We have seen that such allocative processes occur on the basis of students' perceived race. Studies in the United States point to the greater vulnerability to exclusion of racial minority students, resulting in disproportionate numbers dropping out of school without qualifications (Fine, 1991). Studies in Britain have reached similar conclusions. Gillborn's (1990) study showed how subtle mechanisms of exclusion operated in the classroom and how individual teachers were able to affect the quality of students' educational experience by the relationships they built with them. These relationships were particularly affected by the assumptions teachers held about black students and led to their disproportionate exclusion from school.

The origins of relationships of this kind can be found in history: in the mediaeval superstitions and beliefs about 'Others'; in the deeply rooted class structures of British society and, importantly, in the legacies of slavery and colonialism which embedded doctrines of white supremacy in the culture (Rattansi, 1992). In post-colonial times, the presence in the 'Mother Country' of the colonial 'Other' perpetuated these boundaries and divisions along racial lines (Blair and Cole, 2000). I argue that the assumptions held of black (male) students generate fears and anxieties in teachers which have their origins in this cultural history. The experience of black students thus goes beyond mere labelling and extends to a pattern of demonising and criminalising black young people. People's values and beliefs are hugely influential in helping, singly or collectively, to create an institutional environment in which diversity is recognised, accepted and catered for, or which reflects and reproduces the educational and long term interests of a few.

Pressures of the school market

The choices for schools are less straightforward. Schools work within particular contexts and constraints. In England and Wales the Education Reform Act introduced a competitive market model of education which has placed schools under such pressure that for many teachers, their job has become a matter of coping or survival strategies (Woods, 1984; Hargreaves, 1984).

One way schools cope with pressure is by expelling children from school. Schools, and in particular headteachers, have been placed in a dilemma by having to meet statutory demands that have no accompanying resources to aid them (Grace, 1995). But we have seen that school managers are not helpless victims of these demands and can, with enlightened leadership, avoid some of the consequences of these constraints. Levels of student exclusion vary from school to school and this is not always related to the students' socio-economic background (Blair and Bourne, 1998).

In the DfEE study, we identified listening to students and respecting their views as a crucial factor in preventing poor discipline. Teachers were made aware of what mattered to the students and could discuss academic concerns with them, as well as the kind of school community they wanted to create. Working together, a school ethos can be built in which respect and responsibility inform the behaviour of staff and students alike. The studies on which this book is based identify certain factors which shape the inclusive school.

Making education inclusive

School ethos

Every school has a culture or ethos. It either looks outwards towards the children and their parents as the main source of disciplinary problems, or it looks inwards to find ways of providing equal access to education for all children, notwithstanding the pressures of the national curriculum and school league tables. I have argued that the outward focus thwarts any efforts to find bold or imaginative ways of catering for the different needs of students, whereas the inward focus is reflexive and seeks different ways of solving problems within the school. It is necessary to reflect, for example, on why black students have been consistently over-represented in exclusions even in times of comparatively little pressure. Also why some schools maintain low or zero rates of permanent exclusion whereas others continue to exclude many children.

School leadership

The people in positions of authority in a school – the headteacher, governors and teachers – determine whether a school will be democratic or hegemonic. Creating a vision of a democratic school is generally down to the headteacher. Through their personal leadership, they can develop a particular vision and goal for the school. A great deal depends on their ideological orientation towards young people and towards education. A 'business as usual' headteacher is, as we have seen, more likely to conform to traditional definitions of schooling and therefore more likely to exclude students who do not fit in, than one who places the diverse needs of the students at the centre of school processes. The case study of Central City Comprehensive illustrated some of the processes which might affect or exacerbate the vulnerable position of black students. It has been contrasted with Catholic High School, serving an area of immense social deprivation, where the headteacher had a wholly different ideological orientation. She sought to keep students in school and took responsibility for providing the support and moral education that would prepare them for a stable and responsible life after school.

All the students were considered to have special needs but some were seen to be in need of especial support and help from adults. The headteacher and teachers believed that children in the care of the school should not have to pay for the pressures of government demands and constraints with their futures and that those in authority should do everything in their power to keep students in school and learning.

The role of teachers

The studies point to the individual and collective responsibility teachers have for their students. The theoretical framework supports the findings that effective teachers of black students are those who keep students motivated and feel that they themselves must take responsibility for any breakdown of discipline in their classrooms (Haberman, 1995). In other words, these are the teachers who do not seek to blame the parents and children for what happens in the classroom. They can see how students' learning could be affected by negative assumptions and indifference to their individual needs. This is not to deny that children are affected by factors outside school, in the family and the neighbourhood. The case of Aurin at Catholic School illustrated how students can become vulnerable because of aspects of their home or social environments.

The point is that teachers can do a great deal to mitigate the effects of external factors. A team approach to dealing with difficult students was shown to be of far greater benefit to the students themselves and ultimately to the school community and society, than their downright rejection through exclusion.

Teachers' ideological orientation

Interviews with teachers confirmed findings by researchers such as Martin Haberman (1995) and Gloria Ladson-Billings (1994) which show how teachers' ideological orientation towards their students affects their relations with students and their effectiveness as teachers. Effective teachers of minority group students recognised how severely they could disadvantage students, both individually and collectively, because of their culture or ethnicity

They were alert to the assumptions held about specific groups of students and aware of the unfair processes and practices operating against them. The teachers confirmed Ladson-Billings' view that black students respond well to teachers who understand and respect them as people and respect their cultures. Effective teachers were those who were willing to take personal responsibility for the behaviour and attainment of their students and who did not blame the students' families or cultures whenever things went wrong.

Regardless of whether or not they had themselves been excluded from school, the overwhelming response of black students to their *over-representation* in exclusions was that it was the result of unfair treatment. But they did not deny that there were certain black students who broke rules, some who posed particular disciplinary challenges to teachers, some who were a threat to other students. What these students objected to was what they experienced as the undifferentiated way in which they were perceived by teachers. This did not happen to white students whose misdemeanours were assessed and judged individually and not assumed to be part of a white racial or cultural pathology or repertoire.

Racial stereotyping

Black students were particularly angered by the stereotypes which, they felt, shaped teachers' negative judgements of them. Some white teachers, they asserted, held a collective image of black students – male or female – as thieves, with the result that black students were singled out for suspicion when anything went missing in the school. Teachers were also said to regard black students as aggressive and violent and to feel particularly threatened when they saw them – especially males – gathered together. Groups of black boys signalled trouble. Because black students were generally constructed by white teachers as 'tough' and threatening (Sewell, 1997), the students I spoke to believed that they were more likely to retain high visibility, especially in situations of conflict with teachers (Connolly, 1995). Students catalogued their experiences of general exclusion or abuse by teachers, and were articulate about the likelihood that their being stereotyped by teachers denied them equal access to the benefits of school. They saw teacher attitudes of this negative kind as likely to instigate or aggravate conflict. There was nothing biologically or culturally distinctive about black students which made them a particular problem for schools. The problem was that teachers perceived a *collective* difference and constructed it as a problem. This created an environment which effectively set black students up to fail, in both behavioural and academic terms, in ways which do not arise for white students.

Peer group cultures

Black students and white teachers were agreed on one thing: the influence of the peer group was powerful. But agreement ended there. The students and some teachers believed that the involvement of black young people in peer group cultures did not make them more vulnerable than their white counterparts to peer group influence. But they did accept that there were distinct adolescent styles associated more with black young people which were typically viewed as being more hostile to the priorities of schooling than the adolescent cultures of white students. The greater visibility of black students in peer group cultures was in part the result of a complex combination of racial and gender stereotyping by whites in schools, both teachers and students. The failure in relations was seen to lie in the teachers' inability to understand the specific manner in which these cultures influenced young people and in their inability to engage effectively with them. The problem referred to by headteacher Mr Friend, of what he saw as the poor social skills of black students, may arise when white teachers fail to understand black cultural and youth styles.

The teaching and learning environment

The teaching and learning environment was important both for relations between the different ethnic groups in the school, and for determining the behaviour and academic success of black – and indeed all – students. Relationships with individual teachers were, however, crucial to the students, who largely associated their experiences with particular individuals rather than the institution as a whole. So it was not unusual to hear students say that they liked their school and were happy there, but to single out the teachers who marred their enjoyment of school or hampered their success. Conversely, they gave examples of teachers whom they defined as 'good' – those they saw as operating fairly at all times, encouraging and motivating all students and, importantly, being culturally inclusive in their teaching.

Schools use a range of strategies for creating an environment in which good relations prevail, where there is a sense of community and where students respect and enjoy learning. Such an atmosphere can only be created by a staff which is united, committed to students, has clear goals and who support each other in working for the interests of the students. At Station Junior School (LEA study), clear structures existed for all aspects of the school, particularly the area of discipline, so that staff, students and parents were aware of how the school operated and what the expectations were for all the members of the school community. Levels of behaviour and relevant sanctions were clearly understood by everyone and had to be applied consistently across the school. Students knew what was expected of them and could be confident that staff would be consistent and fair at all times.

In some schools, close partnerships were formed between the school and local businesses as a way of interesting students in the outside world of work and providing additional role models who encouraged and motivated them. In some schools, in-service training in conflict resolution, mediation and student counselling were provided for all teachers to help prevent exclusion. There are many such examples of schools which try to transform their own culture for the benefit of all.

Where a particular group in a school stands out in any way, for example, as underachieving or over-excluded, it is important that discussions about the causes of the problem take place with the students, their parents and staff. Parents and students need to be carefully listened to so as to determine whether there are discrepancies between what they see as the problem and what the school thinks it is. In some secondary schools, the staff had 'Away Days' with groups of students to talk about the students' needs and views, and to involve them in drawing up Codes of Behaviour for the school. Students in some schools were consulted on important curriculum issues, such as single sex teaching, or asked to evaluate lessons. Parents and local communities were also consulted and involved in important policy issues, for example drawing up anti-discriminatory policies. A strategy used in one school was to monitor a particular group's progress in order to clarify what the various elements of a problem – say, underachieving – might be. This helped to illuminate the differences between the problems individual students had and those affecting the whole group. Monitoring individual and group student progress might throw light on the relationships between individual teachers and students and thus help to highlight areas in which teachers themselves might need help and support in their work.

Mentoring

A team approach to mentoring has been effective in some schools. Teachers have found ways of supporting students who appear at risk of exclusion by using a teacher the student likes as a mentor or bringing in an outsider. But although outside mentors can be valuable, it seems to signal a failure by the school to create an environment in which students feel that the adults already in the school are their role models and that they can get the help and support they need from them. Outside mentoring can certainly have advantages, not least in academic outcomes, and where mentors are found for students from all ethnicities because of the particular benefits offered by such partnerships, the strategy should not be discounted. But when only black students are selected for mentoring and mentors are found only from their own communities (which is not to decry the racial/ethnic matching in mentoring schemes), it nevertheless seems to me to give out a message equivalent to that of Supplementary Schools, signalling failure by mainstream schools to provide adequately for black students.

Other structures of support may need to be put in place depending on the severity of a student's problems. The way the Irish student at Catholic School was helped is a simple example of effective intervention that did not require extra human or financial resources.

Empowering parents

The parents of excluded students were often angered by the injustices they believed their children endured. When their children were in conflict with the school they felt powerless to influence the outcomes and compelled to accept whatever decision was taken. They felt they were wholly excluded, and were frustrated by their inability to communicate effectively with the school, or they felt intimidated and cowed by the staff's lack of understanding or downright hostility. Some felt demeaned by the way teachers talked to them, or that the teachers' interactions with them were informed by racial stereotypes. They endorsed the view that stereotypes were a problem in teachers' dealings with black students and that these contributed to the level of confrontation. These dynamics hindered communication and left parents feeling helpless and confused.

The culture of the school affects its relationship with parents. Positive interactions are generated in a welcoming atmosphere that gives parents a sense of belonging, not one where parents are made to feel that they are intruding or wasting teachers' time. Parents resent being ignored when they visit the school or left waiting for long periods. One parent reported that when, through no fault of her own, she arrived fifteen minutes late for a meeting with a teacher, she found that he had already gone home whereas she was once kept waiting for twenty minutes by the same teacher because he was in a meeting that was running late.

Parents will feel most empowered to work with the school if they can be convinced that it has a genuine open door policy. They want to feel that they are working in equal partnership with the school for the good of their children. They need clear channels of communication with no room for misunderstanding and the reassurance that their concerns matter to the teachers and headteacher. Setting aside space for groups of parents to meet and share their views and ideas for improvement was found in one school to be a catalyst for black parents taking an active interest in and joining the school's governing body.

Recommendations

Black students were over-represented in exclusions long before the 1986 Education Reform Act. They are over-represented not only because they are likely to be randomly distributed amongst those most vulnerable to exclusion such as the children deemed to have special educational needs, or children in care or in another category identified by the DfEE as 'children with problems', but because they are subjected to school processes which are mediated by race, class and gender. Only when these processes are acknowledged and attacked will the effective criminalisation (NACRO, 1998) of black male students and the disregard for their human rights come to a stop.

This is not an easy process, but it is possible. There follow recommendations which could mitigate and ultimately even end the long history of excluding students from school and instead prepare them for assuming their rights and responsibilities as citizens. These recommendations apply to all schools and all students. But a 'colour-blind' approach is unacceptable, since account must be taken of the powerful effects on students of racism and discrimination.

The Role of Government

• There is a clear need for governments to take heed of the research accounts which detail the causes of teacher stress and to resolve the tensions and conflicts created for teachers by the growing gap between the cognitive and affective aspects of teaching.

• The perspectives of everyone involved in education need to be listened to with care. What schooling means today needs to be clearly defined, taking into account the students' experience of school.

- An 'inclusive education' must of necessity take into account the views and perspectives of students and include them in solutions to the problems which affect them. Young people today are more independent, more informed, more technically competent and more aware than ever before.

- It is time to re-define and re-structure schools in line with economic requirements, certainly, but also in keeping with the cultures and requirements of young people today. The way schools are structured and managed needs to be brought up to date instead of continuing to respond to twenty-first century demands according to nineteenth century methods. The re-constructed, relevant and up-to-date education system must have at its heart the moral, spiritual, physical and emotional develop-ment of children and young people – and not only in political rhetoric. Governments need to supply the means and remove the obstacles to its practical realisation.

Initial Teacher Education

The education of teachers needs to be aligned with these changes. Teacher education, too, needs to be brought into the twenty-first cen-tury and made relevant to the development of students. If teaching is to embrace issues of rights, citizenship and social justice, teachers need to be encouraged to:

- undertake personal exploration of their own values and beliefs. Potential teachers should be encouraged to examine their per-sonal attitudes towards young people and the reasons for them, and to understand the implications of these attitudes for students.

- learn about 'difference' and diversity, about the environment and global responsibility

- be given skills training for teaching these issues and for teaching in multi-ethnic contexts so that they can empathise with the dif-ferent concerns of their students

- be able to recognise the ethnic and racial underpinnings of social discourses and how they disadvantage certain groups of students within school and society

- gain an understanding of the historical relationship between black communities and the educational system in Britain. New teachers need to understand how racism operates and how various ethnic groups are differentially positioned within society. No potential teacher should leave college without some preparation for dealing with racial, sexual, homophobic and other forms of harassment

- receive skills training in understanding and dealing with adolescents

- take a humanisitc approach to teaching and engage with the interests of young people

- be able to deal with conflict in the classroom and school

- provide lessons that are appealing and interesting and nurture in students a desire to learn plus the thrill of acquiring new knowledge.

Schools

Schools need to develop a culture in which the welfare of every student is placed before the competitive image of the school. It means that schools will:

- recognise the vulnerability of students

- recognise that students might have particular problems relating to their backgrounds or families which require a sympathetic and compassionate approach rather than a condemnatory approach that puts students at risk by excluding them from school

- find ways of supporting vulnerable students

- create a school culture which recognises the essential role of the school in providing moral and spiritual guidance to students, and does not abrogate the school's responsibility by problematising the communities and families of the students

- create an environment in which good relations prevail and students can respect and enjoy learning

- establish and maintain a negotiated, fair and consistent behaviour policy so that students know what is expected of them and can expect the staff to be consistent and fair

- provide in-service training on conflict resolution, mediation and student counselling

- make clear to everyone how concerns and grievances are pursued so that justice is seen to be done

- monitor academic progress by gender and ethnicity and take positive action to reverse underachievement of any one group

- review the results of gender and ethnic monitoring and develop a whole-school policy accordingly.

Consultation

Consultation can only be real, and trusted, if the following procedures obtain:

- If one group, say, is underachieving or over-excluded, discussions are held with the students, parents and staff to deal with discrepancies in perceptions of the problem and explore ways forward.

- Students are involved in important policy issues, for example concerning student behaviour.

- Parents and local communities are consulted and involved in policy issues, for example, on sex education or anti-discrimination.

- Staff demonstrate a clear desire to listen to parents and students and take steps to deal with their concerns.

- School governors are involved in policy initiatives and are given specialist governor training on issues that relate to exclusion.

The Headteacher

Headteachers need to:

*   involve all staff in defining the aims and creating a vision for the school, centred on the learning and emotional needs of the students

*   provide sensitive and diplomatic leadership on sensitive issues such as race.

*   allow for open discussion among staff about their fears, anxieties and ideological differences, ensuring that nobody feels excluded or victimised

*   draw on the skills and talents of staff or involve external consultants to help with matters they find difficult to handle

*   know the students, their ethnic, cultural and religious affiliations

*   consult with parents and students to understand their different backgrounds and views and take these into account when drawing up policies

*   make it known to parents that the school is on their and their children's side

The headteacher of Catholic School was clear that the problems in the school could not be resolved unless the problems which beset the black students were understood and dealt with. She insisted that dealing with the issues that affected the black students would reveal the problems and faults in the system as a whole. The Chair of Governors observed:

'The Headteacher has a good understanding of the needs of black pupils, particularly boys. She tries to see where they are coming from and uses strategies which reduce conflict, and talks through with them about using strategies which avoid conflict with teachers. She's been criticised by some staff as favouring black pupils, but in fact she tries to understand where all pupils are coming from. She may need to spend longer with black boys because of the particular experiences of black boys and the history of white staff feeling that black boys are a threat. She treats them as young adults rather than 'naughty children', and gives them equal treatment recognising that she cannot treat all pupils 'the same' because of different experiences. She does not automatically take the side of either the teacher or the pupil, but she is able to see the pupils' point of view.'

- seek the views of parents when drawing up policies

- believe in what they are doing and ensure that it is for the benefit of all students

- be clear about the reasons for each strategy or action and how it will promote the united goals of the school.

Teachers

- Teachers need to believe in the behavioural and academic potential of their students.

- Treat students with respect. The way difficult and challenging students are handled can make all the difference to their behaviour.

- Power struggles with students should be avoided.

- Bullying or humiliating students creates fear rather than respect and mitigates against their learning.

- A strategy used by one teacher was to take time to get to know each of her students and find out something about their individual needs and their family backgrounds as early in the year as possible. She was then able to establish the kind of support each student needed and to devise ways of working with them which made that student feel that the teacher cared in a personal way about him/her. This meant making contact with the parents and agreeing a programme or agenda to help the student

- Black students are aware of the stereotypes held of them and it is for the teachers to demonstrate that they do not subscribe to stereotyped views.

- Give positive attention and quality time to those who are generally or occasionally difficult

- Praise and positive affirmation is more effective than reprimands

- Reflect upon who is praised and who is reprimanded or put down

> In one school teachers found that black boys were underachieving in mathe-matics so they set up a mentoring system whereby each maths teacher took responsibility for one or more of the black boys in Year 10. Each teacher encouraged, cajoled, monitored and set targets for their mentees, working with parents to make sure that the boys were given space and time for homework and that the homework was done well and handed in on time. As all students had a tutor to whom they could go for support and 'failing' white students were included in the scheme, the targeting of this group of black students was not obvious to them or the rest of the students. The support and personal show of interest significantly improved the maths results of the target group. What appeared most important in motivating them was the communication by teachers of their confidence in them.

- Show personal interest in students. No student wants to be given special attention because they are black, but it is important to communicate caring for each student regardless of race. This entails examining one's own attitudes towards issues of race.

- Make conscious efforts to treat students with respect

- Be informed about how race may affect exclusions or academic achievement in the school and support students in the groups known to be vulnerable to failure or exclusion.

- Teachers should develop the potential students have in specific fields, informing and encouraging them to develop their interest and indicating the relevant career possibilities. Sometimes it takes no more than the personal interest of an adult to make learning interesting and relevant to a student, particularly one who is not normally accustomed to such attention.

> One teacher built on a black student's football expertise as a way of motivating him. He watched him play, talked with him about his passion and about the im-portance of academic qualifications even if the student should achieve a career as a footballer. Importantly, this teacher asked his colleagues to take an interest in and encourage the student by motivating him to work at his academic subjects. The student was generally known to be a disruptive element in the classroom but this approach was reported to calm him down considerably and make him more interested in his work.

Working with Parents

As we have seen, white working class and minority ethnic group parents often feel intimidated and powerless in the face of difficulties or conflict with the school. It is up to the school to overcome this problem by using approaches that are known to be effective:

- Make clear to parents what the school's expectations of them are. These expectations should be realistic.

- Try to establish why certain parents never attend Parents' Evenings.

- Ask: 'What are we, the school, doing that keeps certain groups of parents away?' and take corrective action.

- Advise black parents accurately about the academic progress of their children, not only about their behaviour.

- Welcome the initiative of parents who come to discuss issues about their children's schooling.

- Ensure that parents who come to discuss their children are accorded time, privacy, attention and consideration.

For many schools, success in introducing new initiatives or changing the culture of the institution may take a long time. But for change to take place at all requires an examination of the way things are done now, the willingness to think and do things differently and the courage to persevere. The studies on which this book is based have shown time and again that the success or otherwise of a school as a learning community depends on the ethos and environment created by the management team and the staff. The leadership of the school determines whether the students' education is inclusive or selective. Every headteacher must ask: 'What kind of leadership do I offer and whose interests does it serve?' The ability to empower students and create a genuine sense of community in the school depends on how this question is answered.

Bibliography

Advisory Council for Education, (1993) *Investigations into Exclusions*, London, ACE

Apple, M. (1988) *Teachers and Text: A Political Economy of Class and Gender Relations in Education*, New York, Routledge

Apple, M. (1990) *Ideology and Curriculum*, New York, Routledge

Apple, M. (1996) *Cultural Politics and Education*, New York, Teachers College Press

Aronowitz, S. and Giroux, H.A. (1985) *Education Under Siege: The Conservative, Liberal and Radical Debate over Schooling*, South Hadley, MA, Bergin and Garvey

Ball, S. (1987) *The Micro-Politics of the School: Towards a Theory of School Organisation*, London, New York, Methuen

Ball, S. (ed) (1990) *Foucault and Education: Discipline and Knowledge*, London, Routledge

Beckett, K. (1997) *Making Crime Pay: Law and Order in Contemporary American Politics*, New York, Oxford University Press

Becker, H.S. (1963) *Outsiders: Studies in the Sociology of Deviance*, New York, The Free Press

Best, R. (1994) Teachers' Supportive Roles in Secondary Schools: a case study and discussion, in *Support for Learning*, Vol 9 (4), November

Beynon, J. (1989) 'A School for Men': An Ethnographic Case Study of Routine Violence in Schooling, in Walker, S. and Barton, L. (eds) *Politics and the Processes of Schooling*, Open University Press

Blair, M. (1994a) Interviews with Black Families, in Cohen, R., Hughes, M., Ashworth, L. and Blair, M. *School's Out: The family Perspective on School Exclusion*, London, Family Service Units and Barnardos

Blair, M. (1994b), Black Teachers, Black Students and Education Markets, in *Cambridge Journal of Education*, Vol .24, pp.277-91

Blair, M. and Bourne, J. (1998) *Making the Difference: Teaching and Learning in Successful Multi-ethnic Schools*, London DfEE

Blair, M. and Gillborn, D. (1999) Facing up to Racism, *Times Educational Supplement*, 5 March

Blair, M., Gillborn, D., Kemp, S., MacDonald, J. (1999) Institutional Racism, Education and the Stephen Lawrence Inquiry, in *Education and Social Justice*, Vol.1 (3), Summer

Blair, M.(2001) The Education Of Black Children: why do some schools do better than others? in R.Majors (ed) *Educating Our Black Children*, London, Falmer

Blair, M. and Cole, M. (2000) Racism and Education: the Imperial Legacy, in M.Cole (ed) *Human Rights, Education and Equality*, London, Falmer

Blase, J. and Blase, J. (1994) *Empowering Teachers: What Successful School Principles do*, Newbury Park, CA. Corwin

Blase, J. and Anderson, G. (1995) *The Micropolitics of Educational Leadership*, London, Cassell

Blythe, E. and Milner, J. (1994), Exclusion from School and Victim-blaming in *Oxford Review of Education*, Vol. 20, No.3, pp.293-306

Booth, T. Ainscow, M. Dyson, A. (1997), Understanding Inclusion and Exclusion in the English Competitive Education System, in *International Journal of Inclusive Education*. Vol.1, No 4, 337-355

Bottery, M. (1999), Education Under the New Modernisers: an agenda for centralisation, illiberalism and inequality, in *Cambridge Journal of Education*, Vol.29, pp.103-120

Bourne, J., Bridges, L. and Searle, C. (1994) *Outcast England: How Schools Exclude Black Children*, London, Institute of Race Relations

Bowles, S. and Gintis, H. (1976) *Schooling in Capitalist America*, New York, Basic Books

Boyd, C. (1999), *The Pupil Exclusion Maze: more answers than questions*, London, QEC Publications

Brah, A. (1992) Difference, Diversity and Differentiation, in J. Donald and A. Rattansi (eds) *Race, Culture and Difference*, London, Sage

Brah, A. and Minhas, R. (1985), Structural racism or cultural differences: Schooling for Asian girls in G. Weiner (ed) *Just a Bunch of Girls*, Milton Keynes, Open University Press

Bramhall, P. (1995) Exclusion of Pupils: the Law, Conference talk, University of York.

Brandt, G.(1990) *The Realization of Anti-Racist Teaching*, Lewes, Falmer

Bridges, L. (1994) Tory Education: exclusion and the black child, in *Race and Class*, Vol.36, No.1, pp33-48

Broadfoot, P. and Osborn, M. with Gilly, M. and Paillet, A. (1988) What Professional Responsibility Means to Teachers:national contexts and classroom constants, in *British Journal of Sociology of Education*, Vol, 9.(3) 265-287

Brophy, J. and Good, T. (1974) *Teacher-Student Relationships:causes and consequences*, New York. Holt, Rhinehart and Winston

Brown, B. (1998) *Unlearning Discrimination in the Early Years*, Stoke-on-Trent, Trentham Books

Bryan, B., Dadzie, S., and Scafe, S. (1984) *The Heart of the Race: Black Women's Lives in Britain*, London, Virago

Bryk, A., Lee, V. and Holland, P. (1993) *Catholic Schools and the Common Good*, Cambridge, Mass. Harvard University Press

Cashmore, E. and Troyna, B. (eds) (1982) *Black Youth in Crisis*, London, Allen and Unwin

Cavadino, M. and Dignan, J. (1997) *The Penal System: An Introduction*, London, Sage.

Chevannes, M. and Reeves, F. (1987) The Black Voluntary School Movement: definition, context and prospects, in Troyna, B. (ed) *Racial Inequality in Education*, London, Tavistock

Christian, B. (1996) Camouflaging Race and Gender, in *Representations*, No.55 Summer 1996, pp.120-128.

Clark, C.M. (1995) *Thoughtful Teaching*, New York, Cassell

Coard, B. (1971) *How the West Indian Child is made Educationally Sub-Normal in the British School System, London*, New Beacon Books

Cohen, R., Hughes, M., Ashworth, L. and Blair, M. (1994) *Schools Out: The Family Perspective on School Exclusion*, London, Family Service Units and Barnardos

Cohen, P. (1992), It's racism what dunnit': hidden narratives in theories of racism, in Donald, J. and Rattansi, A.(eds) *Race, Culture and Difference*, London, Sage

Commission for Racial Equality (1984) *Birmingham Local Authority and Schools-Referral and exclusion of Pupils: Report for a formal investigation*, London, CRE

Commission for Racial Equality (1997) *Exclusion from School and Racial Equality,* London, CRE

Commission for Racial Equality, Phil Barnet, conference speech, Cambridgeshire, April 2000

Connolly, P. (1994) Racism, anti-racism and masculinity: Contextualising racist incidents in the primary school. Paper presented to International Sociology of Education Conference, University of Sheffield.

Connolly, P. (1995) Boys will be Boys? Racism, Sexuality and the Construction of Masculine Identities amongst Infant Boys, in Holland, J. and Blair, M. *Debates and Issues in Feminist Research and Pedagogy*, Clevedon, Multilingual Matters

Cooper, P., Upton, G. and Smith, C. (1991) Ethnic minority and gender distribution among staff and pupils in facilities for pupils with emotional and behavioural difficulties in England and Wales, in *British Journal of Sociology of Education*, 12, 1, pp.77-94

Corrigan, S.Z. (1996) Classroom Interaction and Management and the Possible Role of Trait Attribution in Classrooms with Diverse Students, (Paper presented at the Annual meeting of the American Educational Research Association, New York)

Cullingford, C. and Morrison, J. (1997) Peer Group Pressure Within and Without School, in *British Educational Research Journal*, 23 (1) 61-80

Currie, E. (1998) *Crime and Punishment in America*, New York, Henry Holt

Curtin, P. (1968) *The Image of Africa*, London, MacMillan

Curtis, T.E. and Bidwell, W.W (1977) *Curriculum and Instruction for Emerging Adolescents*, New York, Addison

Department for Education (1992) *Exclusions. A Discussion Paper*, London, DFE

Department for Education and Employment (1999) *Circular 10/99 Social Inclusion: Pupil Support*, London, DfEE

Delgado, R. and Stefanic, J.(eds) (1997) *Critical White Studies: Looking Behind the Mirror*, Philadelphia, Temple University Press

Driver, G. (1979) Classroom Stress and School Achievement: West Indian Adolescents and their Teachers, in Saifullah Khan, V. (ed) *Minority Families in Britain: Support and Stress*, London, Macmillan

Duncan, G.A.(1996) Space, Place and the Problematic of Race: Black Adolescent Discourse as Mediated Action, in *Journal of Negro Education*, Vol.65, No.2 Spring.

Edelman, M. (1994) *Wasting America's Future: The Children's Defense Fund Report on the costs of child poverty*, Boston, Beacon Press.

Eggleston, S.J., Dunn, D.K. and Anjali, M. (1986) *Education for Some: the Educational and Vocational Experiences of 15-18 year old Members of Minority Ethnic Groups*, Stoke-on-Trent, Trentham.

Ellison, Ralph (1965) *Invisible Man*, London, Penguin, third edition

Essed, P. (1990) *Understanding Everyday Racism*, London, Sage

Eysenck, H.J.(1971) *Race, Intelligence and Education*, London, Temple Smith

Fanon, F. (1970) *Black Skins, White Masks*, London, Paladin

Figueroa, P. (1991) *Education and the Social Construction of Race*, London, Routledge

Fine, M. (1991) *Framing Dropouts: Notes on the Politics of an Urban Public High School*, New York, SUNY Press

Fordham, S. (1996) *Blacked Out: Dilemmas of Race, Identity, and Success at Capital High*, University of Chicago Press

Foster, P. (1990) *Policy and Practice in Multicultural and Antiracist Education*, London, Routledge

Foucault, M. (1979) *Discipline and Punishment*, transl. Alan Sheridan, Vintage Books

Freire, P. (1985) *The Politics of Education: Culture, Power and Liberation* (D. Macedo, trans) New York, Bergin and Garvey

Fuller, M. (1984) Black girls in a London Comprehensive, in Hammersley, M. and Woods, P. (eds) *Life in School: The Sociology of Pupil Culture*, Milton Keynes, Open University Press

Galloway, D. Mortimore, P. and Tutt, N. (1982) *Schools and Disruptive Pupils,* London, Longman

Gandy, O.H. (1998) *Communication and Race: a Structural Perspective,* London, Arnold

Gillborn, D. (1990) *Race Ethnicity and Education*, London, Unwin Hyman

Gillborn, D. (1995a) *Racism and Antiracism in Real Schools*, Buckingham, Open University Press

Gillborn, D. (1995b) Racism and Exclusions from School: case studies in the denial of educational opportunities (Paper prepared for the European Conference on Educational Research (ECER) University of Bath

Gillborn, D. (1997) Young, Black and Failed by school: the market, education reform, and black students, in *International Journal of Inclusive Education*, Vol. 1, No.1, pp 65-87.

Gillborn, D. and Gipps, C. (1996) *Recent Research on the Achievement of Ethnic Minority Pupils*, London, HMSO

Gilman, S. (1992) Black Bodies, White Bodies: toward an iconography of female sexuality in late nineteenth-century art, medicine and literature, in Donald, J. and Rattansi, A. *Race, Culture and Difference*, London, Sage

Gilroy, P. (1987) *There ain't no black in the Union Jack*, London, Hutchinson

Gilroy, P. (1992) The end of antiracism, in Donald, J. and Rattansi, A. *Race, Culture and Difference*, London, Sage

Giroux, H.A. (1989) *Schooling for Democracy – Critical Pedagogy in the Modern Age*, London, New York, Routledge

Goldberg, E. and Evans, L. (1998) *The Prison Industrial Complex and the Global Economy*, AGIT Press

Goodlad, J. (1984) *A Place Called School: Prospects for the Future*, New York, McGraw-Hill.

Gordon, P. (1988) Black people and the criminal law: rhetoric and reality, in *International Journal of Sociology of Law,* Vol.16, pp.295-313

Gottfredson, D.C. Gottfredson, G.D. and Hybl, L.G. (1993) Managing Adolescent Behaviour: A Multiyear, Multischool Study, in *American Educational Research Journal* 30 (1) 179-215

Grace, G. (1995) *School Leadership: Beyond Education Management*, London Falmer

Green, D. (1982) Teachers' influence on the self-concept of different ethnic groups, unpublished PhD thesis, cited in Troyna, B. (1993) *Racism and Education*, Buckingham, Open University Press.

Greenfield, W.D. (1991) The Mocropolitics of Leadership in an Urban Elementary School, in Blase, J. (ed) *The Politics of Life in schools: Power, Conflict and Co-operation*, Newbury Park, Sage

Haberman, M. (1995) *Star Teachers of Children in Poverty*, West Lafayette, Indiana, Kappa, Delta, Pi

Hall, S. (1980) Teaching about Race, in James, A. and Jeffcoate, R. (eds) *The School in the Multicultural Society*, London, Harper

Hall, S. (1984) *Gramsci's Relevance to the Analysis of Racism and Ethnicity*, Unesco, Division of Human Rights and Peace

Hall, S. (1985) Signification, Representation, Ideology: Althusser and the Post-Structuralist Debates, in *Critical Studies in Mass Communication* 2, (2), 91-114

Hall, S. (1992) 'New Ethnicities' in Donald, J. and Rattansi, A. *Race, Culture and Difference*, London, Sage

Hall, S., Critcher, C., Jefferson, T., Clarke, J. and Roberts, B. (1978), *Policing the Crisis: Mugging, the State, and Law and Order*, N.York, Holmes and Meier Publishers

Hanrahan, N. (1998) Media Bows to Power: Will Mumia's voice be silenced forever? in Burton-Rose, D. (ed) *The Celling of America*, Monroe, Maine, Common Courage Press

Hansen, D. (1997) Being a Good Influence, in Burbules, N. and Hansen, D. *Teaching and its Predicaments*, New York, Westview Press

Hargreaves, A. (1984) The Significance of Classroom Coping Strategies, in A. Hargreaves and P. Woods, *Classrooms and Staffrooms: The Sociology of Teachers and Teaching*, Milton Keynes, Open University Press.

Hargreaves, A. (1994) *Changing Teachers, Changing Times: Teachers' Work Culture in the Postmodern Age*, London, Cassell

Hargreaves, A., Earl, L., Ryan, J. (1996) *Schooling for Change: Re-inventing Education for Early Adolescents*, London, Falmer

Hargreaves, D., Hester, S.K., and Mellor, F.J. (1975) *Deviance in Classrooms*, London, Routledge

Hayden, C. (1997) *Children Excluded from Primary School: Debates, Evidence, Responses*, Buckingham, Open University Press

Herrnstein, R. and Murray, C. (1994) *The Bell Curve:Intelligence and Class Structure in American Life*, New York, The Free Press

Hill-Collins, P. (1986) Learning from the Outside Within: The Sociological Significance of Black Feminist Thought, in *Social Problems* (33), 6, December, 1986.

Hill-Collins, P. (1990) *Black Feminist Thought*, London, New York, Routledge

Hiro, D. (1971) *Black British, White British*, London, Pelican

Hollinger, D. (1996), Group Preferences, Cultural Diversity and Social Democracy in *Representations*, No.55, Summer, 1996, 31-40.

hooks, b. (1990) *Yearning: Race, Gender and Cultural Politics*, Boston, MA, South End Press

Hurrell, P. (1995) Do teachers discriminate? Reactions to pupil behaviour in four comprehensive schools, in *Sociology*, Vol.29 (1) pp.59-72.

Imich, A.J. (1994) Exclusion from school: current trends and issues, in *Educational Research*, Vol. 36, No.1, p. 3-11

Institute of Race Relations, (1994) *Outcast England. How Schools Exclude Black Children*, London, IRR

Issues in Race and Education, No.34, Autumn 1981

Jensen, A. (1969) How much can we boost IQ and scholastic achievement? in *Harvard Educational Review*, Vol.39, No1, 1-123

Jones, A. (1987) *Leadership for Tomorrow's Schools*, Oxford, Basil Blackwell

Jones, D. (1994) The genealogy of the urban schoolteacher, in Ball, S. (ed) *Foucault and Education: Disciplines and Knowledge*, London, Routledge

Jones, A. and Myrant, M. (1991) *Trends and Issues 91: Education and Criminal Justice in Illinois*, Illinois Criminal Justice Information Authority, Chicago, IL

Jordan, (1968) *White over Black:American attitudes towards the Negro*, University of Carolina Press

Keddie, N. (1971) Classroom Knowledge, in Young, M.F.D. (ed) *Knowledge and Control: New Directions for the Sociology of Education*, London, Collier-MacMillan

Keddie, N. (1984) Classroom Knowledge, in Hargreaves, A. and Woods, P., *Classrooms and Staffrooms: the Sociology of Teachers and Teaching*, Milton Keynes, Open University Press

King, J. (1998) Dysconcious Racism: Ideology, Identity and Mis-Education in Delagado, R. and Stefanic, J. *Critical White Studies:looking behind the mirror*, Philadelphia, Temple University Press

Ladson-Billings, G. (1994) *The Dreamkeepers: Successful Teachers of African American Children*, S. Francisco, Jossey-Bass Publishers

Lawrence, J. (1984) *Disruptive Children: Disruptive Schools?* London, Longman

Mac an Ghaill, M. (1988) *Young Gifted and Black: Student-Teacher Relations in the Schooling of Black Youth*, Milton Keynes, Open University Press

Mac an Ghaill, M. (1994) *The Making of Men: Masculinities, Sexualities and Schooling*, Buckingham, Open University Press

McCarthy, C. (1990) *Race and Curriculum*, London, Falmer Press

MacDonald, I. John, G. and Bhavnani, R. (1989) *Murder in the Playground, The Burnage Report*, London: Longsight Press

McLaren, P. (1986) *School as a Ritual Performance*, London, Routledge

Majors, R. and Billson, J.M. (1992) *Cool Pose: The Dilemmas of Black Manhood in America*, New York, Lexington Books

Mayet, G.H. (1993) Exclusions and Schools, in *Multicultural Education Review* No.15, Winter, 93/94, pp. 7-9

Maylor, U. (1995) The Experiences of African, Caribbean and South Asian Women in Initial Teacher Education (Unpublished Ph.D. thesis, Open University)

Mickelson, R.A. (1990) The Attitude-Achievement Paradox Among Black Adolescents, in *Sociology of Education* Vol. 63, January, pp.44-61

Milner, D. (1975) *Children and Race*, London, Penguin

Mirza, H. (1992) *Young, Female and Black*, London, Routledge

Mirza, M. (1995) Some ethical dilemmas in fieldwork: feminist and antiracist methodologies, in Griffiths, M. and Troyna, B. (eds) *Antiracism, Culture and Social Justice in Education*, Stoke-on-Trent, Trentham Books

Mortimore, P., Sammons, P., Stoll, L., Lewis, D. and Ecob, R. (1988) *School Matters: the Junior Years*, Wells, Open Books.

NACRO (National Association for the Care and Resettlement of Offenders) (1998) *Children, Schools and Crime*, London, NACRO.

National Union of Teachers (1992) *Survey of Pupil Exclusions*, London, NUT

Nias, J. (1985) Reference Groups in Primary Teaching: Talking, Listening and Identity, in Ball, S. and Goodson, I. *Teachers' Lives and Careers*, London, Falmer

Noguera, P. (1996), Responding to the Crisis Confronting California's Black Male Youth: providing support without furthering marginalization, in *Journal of Negro Education*, Vol. 65, No.2 Spring 1996.

Noguera, P. (1997) Reconsidering the 'Crisis' of the Black Male in America, in *Journal of Social Justice*, Vol.24 (2) pp.147-164

Nottinghamshire County Council, (1991) (Report No. 15/89) *Pupil Exclusions from Nottingham Secondary Schools*, Nottinghamshire County Council Education Department

Oakes, J. (1985) *Keeping Track: How Schools Structure Inequality*, New Haven, CT. Yale University Press

Oakley, A. (1981), Interviewing Women: a contradiction in terms? in Roberts, H. (ed) *Doing Feminist Research*, London, Routledge

Office for Standards in Education (1993) *Exclusions:A Response to the Department for Education Discussion Paper*, London, HMSO

Office for Standards in Education (1996) *Exclusions in Secondary Schools,* London, HMSO

Ogbu, J. (1978) *Minority Education and Caste: the American System in Cross-Cultural Perspective*, New York, Academic Press

Ogbu, J. (1988) Understanding Cultural Diversity and Learning, in *Educational Researcher*, Vol 21, No 8, pp.5-14

Omi, M. and Winant, H. (1993) On the Theoretical Concept of Race, in McCarthy, C. and Crichlow, W. *Race, Identity and Representation in Education*, New York, London, Routledge

Osler, A. and Starkey, H. (1996) *Teacher Education and Human Rights*, London, David Fulton

Osler, A. (1997) *Exclusion from School and Racial Equality*, London, CRE

Osler, A. and Hill, J. (1999) Exclusion from School and Racial Equality: an examination of government proposals in the light of recent research evidence, in *Cambridge Journal of Education*, Vol. 29 (1) pp.33 -62

Parsons, C., Hailes, J., Howlett, K., Davies, A., Driscoll, P. and Ross, L. (1995) *Natonal Survey of Local Education Authorities Policies and Procedures for the Identification of, and Provision for, Children who are out of School by Reason of Exclusion or Otherwise*, London, DfE

Pearson, G. (1983) *Hooligan: a history of respectable fears*, London, Macmillan

Postman, N. (1996) *The End of Education: Redefining The Value of School*, New York, Vintage Books

Rampton, A. (1981) *West Indian Children in our Schools,* London, HMSO

Rattansi, A. (1992) Changing the subject? racism, culture and education, in Donald, J. and Rattansi, A. *Race, Culture and Difference*, London, Sage

Rattansi, A. and Donald, J. (1992) The Question of Racism. *Course Introduction, ED356, Race, Education and Society*, Open University.

Riseborough, G.F. (1984) Teacher Careers and Comprehensive Schooling:An Empirical Study, in A. Hargreaves and P. Woods, *Classrooms and Staffrooms: The Sociology of Teachers and Teaching*, Milton Keynes, Open University Press

Scarman Report (1981) *The Brixton disorders:10-12 April, 1981*, London, HMSO

Scraton, P. Sim, J. and Skidmore, P. (1991) *Prisons Under Protest*, Buckingham, Open University Press

Searle, C. (1997) Demagoguery in Process: authoritarian populism, the press and school exclusions, in *FORUM*, Vol.39, No.1, pp14-19.

Sewell, T. (1997) *Black Masculinity and Schooling*, Stoke-on-Trent, Trentham Books

Sharp, R. and Green, A. (1975) *Education and Social Control: A Study in Progressive Primary Education*, London, Routledge and Kegan Paul

Sharp, R. and Green, A. (1984) Social Stratification in the Classroom, in Hargreaves, A. and Woods, P. *Classrooms and Staffrooms: The Sociology of Teachers and Teaching*, Milton Keynes, Open University Press

Siraj-Blatchford, I. (1991) Access to what? Black students' perceptions of Initial Teacher Education, in *Journal of Access Studies*, Vol. 5, No. 2, pp. 177-187.

Sleeter, C. (1996) How White Teachers Construct Race, in McCarthy, C. and Crichlow, W. *Race, Identity and Representation in Education*, New York, London, Routledge

Small, S. (1983) *Police and People in London: A Group of Young Black People*, London, Policy Studies Institute

Smith, D. and Tomlinson, S. (1989) *The School Effect: A Study of Multiracial Comprehensives*, London, Policy Studies Institute

Social Exclusion Unit (1998) *Truancy and School Exclusion*, London, HMSO

Solomos, J. (1988) *Black Youth, Racism and the State*, Cambridge, Cambridge University Press

Stern, V. (1998) *A Sin Against the Future: Imprisonment in the World*, Penguin Books

Stirling, M. (1992) How Many Pupils are being Excluded? in *British Journal of Special Education*, Vol 19, No 4 pp.128-130

Stirling, M. (1993) A 'Black Mark' Against Him? Why are African-Caribbean Boys Over-Represented in the Excluded Pupil Populations? In *Multicultural Review*, No.15, Winter

The Swann Report, (1985) *Education for All: Report of the Committee of Inquiry into the Education of Children from Minority Ethnic Groups*, London, HMSO.

Tattum, D.P. (1982) *Disruptive pupils in schools and Units*, Chichester, John Wiley

Tizard, B., Blatchford, P., Burke, J., Farquhar, C., and Plewis, I., (1988) *Young Children at School in the Inner City*, Hove, Lawrence Erlbaum Associates

Tomlinson, S. (1984) *Home and School in Multiracial Britain*, London, Batsford

Tonry, M.H. (1995) *Malign Neglect – Race, Crime and Punishment in America*, New York, Oxford University Press

Troyna, B. (1984) Fact or artefact? The 'educational underachievement' of black pupils, in *British Journal of Sociology of Education*, vol.5 (2) pp.153-166

Troyna, B. (1988) Paradigm regained: a critique of 'cultural deficit' perspectives on contemporary educational research, in *Comparative Education*, 24 (3) 273 - 83.

Troyna, B. (1992) Can you see the join? A historical analysis of multicultural and antiracist education policies, in Gill, D., Mayor, B. and Blair, M., *Racism in Education: Structures and Strategies*, London, Sage.

Troyna, B. (1993) *Racism and Education*, Buckingham, Open University Press.

Troyna, B. (1998) 'The whites of my eyes, nose, ears.....': a reflexive account of 'whiteness' in race-related research, in Connolly, P. and Troyna, B., *Researching Racism in Education: Politics, Theory and Practice*, London, Routledge

Troyna, B. and Hatcher, R. (1992) *Racism in Children's Lives: a study of mainly white primary schools*, London, Routledge

Tumim, S. (1997) *The Future of Crime and Punishment*, London, Phoenix

van Dijk, T.A. (1993) Analysing Racism Through Discourse Analysis: Some Methodological Reflections, in Stanfield, J.H. and Rutledge, M.D., *Race and Ethnicity in Research Methods*, Newbury Park, Sage

Walkerdine, V. (1989) *Counting Girls Out*, London, Virago

Wexler, P. (1992) *Becoming Somebody:Towards a Social Psychology of School*, London, Falmer

Wolpe, A. (1988) *Within School Walls: The Role of Discipline, Sexuality and the Curriculum*, London, Routledge

Woods, P. (1984) Teaching for Survival, in A. Hargreaves and P.Woods, (eds) *Classrooms and Staffrooms: The Sociology of Teachers and Teaching*, Milton Keynes, Open University Press

Woods, P. (1990) *The Happiest Days? How Pupils Cope with School*, London, Falmer

Worrall, A. (1997) *Punishment in the Community: The Future of Criminal Justice*, London/New York, Longman

Wright, C. (1987) Black students-white teachers, in Troyna, B. (ed) *Racial Inequality in Education*, London, Routledge

Wright, C. (1992a) Early education: multiracial primary school classrooms, in Gill, D., Mayor, B. and Blair, M. *Racism in Education, Structures and Strategies*, London, Sage

Wright, C. (1992b) *Race Relations in the Primary School*, London, David Fulton

Wright, C., Weekes, D., McGlaughlin, A., and Webb, D., (2000) *Race, Class and Gender in Exclusion from School*, London, New York, Falmer Press

Wright, P. (1998) The Global Economy behind Prison Walls, in Burton-rose, D. (ed) *The Celling of America*, Common Courage Press

Young, J. (1997) Charles Murray and the American Prison Experiment: The Dilemmas of a Libertarian, in Murray, C. (ed) *Does Prison Work?* London IEA

Young, M.F.D. (1971) (ed) *Knowledge and Control: New Directions for the Sociology of Education*, London, Collier-MacMillan

INDEX